# LE CORBUSIER *alive*

# LE CORBUSIER *alive*

Text, Dominique Lyon
Photography, Anriet Denis
Coordination, Olivier Boissière



TERRAIL

*Front cover*
Photomontage: Le Corbusier's profile and stained-glass window of the chapel of Notre-Dame-du-Haut.

*Back cover*
The "Modulor", litography from the *Poème de l'angle droit* (1955).

*Previous page*
Villa La Roche, Paris.

English adaptation: Kathryn Walton-Ward
Notes by: Véronique Donnat


25, rue Ginoux - 75015 Paris - FRANCE
ISBN: 2-87939-238-1
Printed in Italy

# Contents

Le Corbusier has bothered us for a long time. Indeed he had troubled others. Everyone has heard of him, as he was hardly discreet, being perhaps the first architect to have understood (and manipulated) the media. His death – a drowning in the manner of Shelley – did not settle matters: there was a rather pompous funeral ceremony complete with speech by Malraux. The centenary of his birth, marked by countless exhibitions, catalogs and other publications, only added to an overabundant bibliography, which should, under normal circumstances, have closed the chapter for good: embalming the man and his work for eternity.

And yet, critiques and historical studies were keeping a scent of incompleteness afloat. The polemics were calming themselves down slowly, leaving long trails behind, as if well-aired opinions were resigned to please each other. The statue of the Commander was starting to look like a Merz collage; the architect of the century was turning into some sort of hybrid megalomaniac planner, approximate technician, liar, doctrinaire and genius. As for the built work, it seemed to have been nicely tidied into pigeonholes in the form of faded photos, hidden away by exegese, numbed by history, wrapped up in opaque folds of logos. Enough to inspire a whiff of suspicion. What is exactly left today of this handful of heroic buildings displayed for our edification in catalogs and on museum walls? We decided to get to the bottom of things and examine some of these buildings, selecting twenty or so of the best preserved: those still closest to their original state, those who had been spared the onslaughts of time and man.

To talk about such a body of work, we had to spot someone gifted with both freedom of speech and clarity of vision. The lot fell to Dominique Lyon. Lyon is an architect himself – not necessarily an advantage in the case. Luckily for him, he is not from the generation directly after Corbu. He had not been taught unquestioning devotion to the master nor had he been trained to ignore his work or regard it with contempt. Lyon could consider Le Corbusier as he might Palladio – a great man who could still pass on a lesson or two, albeit not literally of course. For the boy (Le Corbusier) and Lyon live in very different times. Le Corbusier lived through a century rocked by violent transformations, caught up in a maelstrom of social upheavals. The young man (Lyon) lives in a period of Western society that is comparatively calm. He glances at the works of Sophie Calle, Bruce Nauman and Roman Signer (also Swiss); he follows the leaps and glides of Merce Cunningham; he delights in Francis Ponge and Valère Novarina; he can whistle any tune by Bob Dylan or Padre Soler. In short, he is a man at home in his era. No blind fate forces him to revolt against his fathers (Nouvel and Gehry) for they love and recognize him, nor to rail against an abusive mother, society, for he is her legitimate son and he only wishes her well. No doubt, Lyon was the man for the job.

A word about the visuals. Above all we wanted them to be new, fresh and unaffected, without the heroics produced by the use of unlikely angles or magical filters. With Anriet Denis we opted for an objective (insofar as such thing exists) viewpoint. Her straightforward and rigorous approach did the rest. After all, "*le jeu savant, correct et magnifique des volumes sous la lumière...*" can serve as a rather good definition for photography. We also needed a certain amount of factual information. That rather thankless task was handled with grace and skill by Véronique Donnat.

So then, we started off, guided by nothing more than our own desire – but with an eye on the weather forecast – subject to no prior chronology or order of importance set by academic criticism. With neither false naivete nor self deception – for we had already come in contact with Le Corbusier before (how could it be otherwise?) and some scattered memories had stuck: waking up in a little classical palazzo in Marseilles, with a rectangular pool watched over by two allegorical figures, the Saône on one side, the Rhône on the other, to set the tone, and towering over it all, the superb silhouette of the Unité d'habitation itself; the satanic story told by Stanley Tigerman about a dinner party of American architects at the restaurant Vagenende in Paris, in the course of which the inimitable Hedjuk expressed the suspicion that La Roche held black masses and that Corbu knew; an elegant soirée in Garches in a villa still haunted by the ghosts of an odd trio, now converted into a condominium; a rainy afternoon on a Jura hill, the little mount in the shape of a pyramid and far from his California home, in his Columbo raincoat, a great architect, under a great black umbrella, mumbling audibly, "It's all fish." It is not easy to cast off the burden of one's culture, however lightweight it may be. Deliberate amnesia is illusory. We merely agreed we would try to remain (relatively) innocent.

So we set out expecting nothing and, as they say quaintly around Neuchâtel, "we were pleasantly disappointed". Disappointed, yes, because what we found bore little resemblance to what we had seen in the faded snapshots and read in countless commentaries. Disappointed, and vaguely furious too, at all that had been concealed from us for ages out of some supposed respect (or disdain perhaps) for something that is immense and unimaginable.

At the risk of trespassing on Lyon's territory, we must proclaim loud and clear that (to use a favorite word of teenagers today) Corbu is awesome. His genius is always somewhere else than expected, it is a virtuoso performance, daring and offhand. It is beautiful, moving, droll, pathetic.

It wears its age well. It stirs the blood and arouses the senses. It fears neither wear nor ruin. It reconciles one with the world. It is optimistic, sublime and, dare one say, sacred. Although when questioned on the subject of his faith, Corbu is said to have answered with a curt, "Leave me alone." The mystery remains.
Faced with that unfathomable question, we went to La Certosa monastery of Florence, which, as everyone knows, is really in Galuzzo on the outskirts of the city and is always referred to – *e chi sa perché ?* – as the Certosa d'Ema. But when we got there, there had been change: giving in to times, the monastery closed on Mondays. Like the Uffizi. So we loitered in front of a closed facade along with a group of nuns, helpless and condemned, just like us, to make do with the booze distilled by the monks according to age-old recipes. Had Le Corbusier bowed to custom and tasted the liqueur? Perhaps not. He was more of an ascetic. His spareness and simplicity resembled that of Francis of Assisi (in Corbu's sketches you can hear the little birds talk). His austerity suited him so well that he wanted everybody to benefit from it. Frugal and exemplary, like the great Toto in Pasolini's *Uccellaci e Uccellini*...
Architecture needs more than beautiful words and pretty images. Le Corbusier's more than any other. You have to wander around it, for the pure delight of it. Go visit Corbu. Go and bathe in its youth, liberty, insolence, sublimity. Go. Run. Corbu is good for you.

Olivier Boissière

**Charterhouse of Florence located in Galuzzo.**

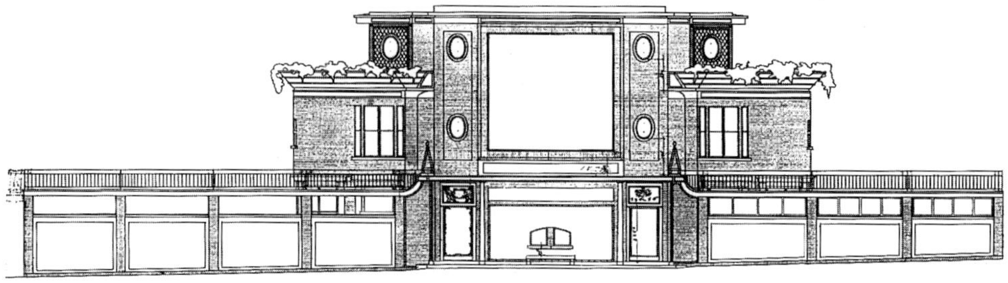

In November 1911, Charles-Edouard Jeanneret came back to La Chaux-de-Fonds (where he was born) after a long journey (Bulgaria, Turkey, Greece, Italy) and he landed three construction contracts. These were the villa Favre-Jacot in Le Locle, the villa Blanche of Jeanneret's parents in 1912 and the villa Schwob in 1916. Charles-Edouard also painted (he showed his work in Neuchâtel and in Paris), and wrote *Voyage d'Orient*. Most importantly, he started his first theoretical studies and projects on the subject of social housing and industrial construction. His credo was "le béton libérateur" (concrete liberates).

As early as February 1912, the young architect boasted of his mastery of reinforced concrete in a letter sent out to regional bankers and industrialists. In 1914, with Zurich architect Du Bois, he imagined the post/slab construction principle "Dom-ino." From Citrohan to Chandigarh, he constantly sought to find new variations and improvements. He first used the concept in 1916 on the home of industrialist Anatole Schwob.

"Neither poor, nor puffed up with shining scales, cement appears there in its structure, where it is useful, like a strong framework, with no more conceit than that of the appearance of bones in the human body that provide feelings of security and beauty for the eyes and the mind." Julien Caron, known as Amédée Ozenfant, adds in *L'Esprit nouveau* (March 1921, No.VI) on the subject of the villa Schwob: "There is no decoration to differentiate one room from another. Here, the volume suffices."

The villa Schwob was a last-ditch struggle against traditional methods and the final project of the young Jeanneret in La Chaux-de-Fonds before he settled in Paris. It concluded his years of travel and training. Its two apses, its cornices and reliefs, its "strangeness" in the eyes of local residents, earned the villa the nickname "villa Turque" (Turkish Villa).

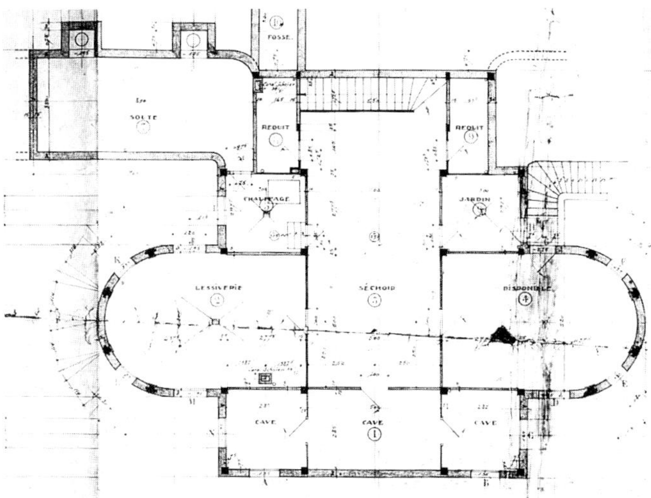

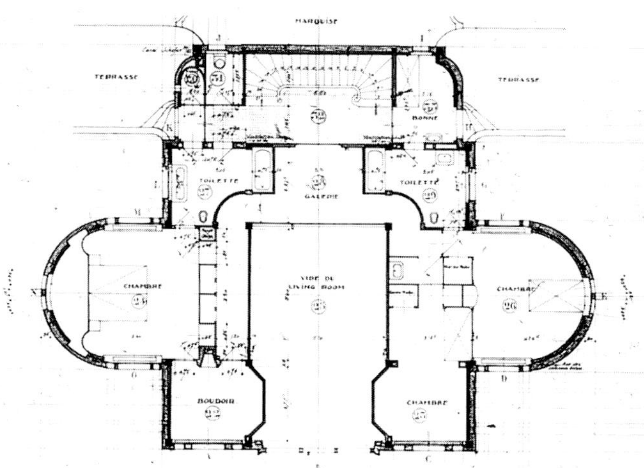

# Villa Schwob

**Project architect:** Charles-Edouard Jeanneret.
**Clients**: Anatole Schwob, Swiss watch industrialist, and his wife Camille.
**Construction dates**: August 1916-September 1917.
**Description:** Family residence, 235 square meters.
**Location**: 167, rue du Doubs in La Chaux-de-Fonds, Neuchâtel, Switzerland.
**Current condition**: Restored in 1957-58 by the Italian architect Angelo Mangiarotti then again in 1987 by the architects Roland and Pierre Studer (from La Chaux-de-Fonds) for the Ebel company. Interior design by Andrée Putman. Today the villa Schwob is the Ebel company's public relations center.

# As the work on the villa Schwob neared

completion, Charles-Edouard Jeanneret left La Chaux-de-Fonds to settle in Paris. Soon after, he chose to take a quite peculiar name: Le Corbusier. This was the first, and not the least, of the many deeds that would contribute to his fame.

In "Le Corbusier," one first hears the article; it is not surprising that the article should precede the noun. However, its presence is intriguing: this assumed name was made up by a man good with words and formulas. What should one make of it?

In French, the definite article introduces the adjectives that history sets aside for those whose accomplishments are outstanding: Alexander the Great, Jack the Ripper, Ivan the Terrible and so forth.

Before a proper name, with no reference to a first name, the article indicates a person whose reputation has been established. Between friends this construction indicates informality, but calling out "Hey, here comes le Le Corbusier!" sounds bad. However, this same device is the mark of great respect that is set aside for exceptionally talented individuals, generally artists whose works are influential: La Callas (Maria Callas), Le Titien (Titian), Le Tintoret (Tintoretto).

To treat oneself with such deference would be ridiculous, but bearing a name which discreetly suggests such distinction is not unpleasant. Le Corbusier took even greater advantage of this since he would refer to himself in the third person. What remains obvious is that an article replaces the first name. Now, the function of the first name is to single out an individual in a line of descendants. By casting this aside, Charles-Edouard placed himself outside any ancestry; he created himself.

Undoubtedly, the feeling that he had made a determining discovery that enabled him to make out a clear new path, inspired the young Jeanneret to give up his patronymic. He was an enterprising young man who was confident in his own ability. He had no time for mistakes, whether his own or those of other people. As soon as he realized that he had the capacity to influence architecture with his truly daring principles, Charles-Edouard Jeanneret shouldered the responsibility of a leading part on the stage of his art form and took on a name intended to strike the public from the outset.

But, Le Corbusier is more than just a theatrical name. It is a generic name – thrown out as a challenge – to be used in everyday language in the same way as brand names: Frigidaire, Vespa. The name carries within itself, perhaps in spite of itself, the idea of a future lineage. One day the Corbusians will come and the noun will become an adjective. Le Corbusier sprang forth from Jupiter's thigh, alone and fully armed. His weapons were architectural principles.

**Facade on the street.**

**Northeastern corner.**

Charles-Edouard Jeanneret finished building the villa Schwob in 1917. He was 31 years old and, thus far, had lived his life well. He had an open-minded artistic education and filled entire notebooks with sketches and notes during trips to Italy, Greece and the Far East. He discovered the modern masters in Vienna (Loos, Wagner, Hoffman), Berlin (Berhens and Gropius), and Paris (Perret). His curiosity led him to mix in various intellectual and artistic circles, circles whose influences were bound to leave him feeling embarrassed and confused. However, whether he became enthusiastic or allowed himself to be impressed, he always retained his critical faculties. He subjected everything to analysis and, thanks to his powers of reflection, these influences quickly wore off.
Thus, he saw architecture as both an art form – a field in which a certain amount of irrationality and passion are expressed by talent – and as an intellectual discipline in which ideas and principles were developed. After the confusion of his formative years, Le Corbusier, concerned with intellectual lucidity and inclined to seek the absolute, wanted his thinking to take a pure form. He appealed to "the truth" to define his architectural principles. His arguments looked to geometry and mathematical harmonies for support. His argumentation calls for the rational thinking of engineers and industrialists. However, truth and reason cannot be summoned if they are not destined to apply to the world as a whole, including objects, machines, buildings, the layout of cities and the organization of everyday

**Terrace on the second level and oculus.**

**Western facade.**

Mezzanine balcony.

*Opposite page:* Living room and glass case with access to the garden.

Office corner.

life. His truth lays claim to universality. As a consequence, the architect who takes care to establish exact principles must view all facets of the world as something to feed on as soon as he senses their purity of spirit. Le Corbusier sees this in boats, cars and aircraft. When he draws a parallel between the Parthenon and a Delage sportscar, the transparent quality of his vision of the world verges on perfection.

The architect becomes a modern artist when he learns how to perceive what the world around him produces and when he gains the ability to transform its products. This involves excessiveness: excessiveness and truth must learn to put up with each other.

When Charles-Edouard Jeanneret built the villa Schwob, his intellectual approach and his artistic quest took routes where the influences of his youth were still visible. The villa is simple as its references come from an area where classicism (as the depository of absolute values) and the "modern" (as the representation of rational values) meet in order to form a modern version of classicism as illustrated by Perret and Hoffman. The villa announces Le Corbusier's style in its combination of exact volumes and the presence of surprising visual elements whose strength lies in the fact that they are outsized. Even today, the villa retains this strangeness. The building is a symmetrical whole constructed by organizing elementary volumes: cylinders and parallelepipeds. The cross-shaped layout flanked by semi-cylindrical apses evokes the design of a basilica. The construction is "rational": a system of posts and concrete beams lightens the construction by reducing the walls to thin partitions. This enables large openings to be made in the facade that make for attractive transparencies. These facades are surfaces without ornamentation, unnecessary layers or additions that would irritate the eye.

The architecture of the villa Schwob is based on the arrangement of simple volumes: it tends toward abstraction. The villa offers a rather neutral background to which Charles-Edouard Jeanneret affixes three oversized elements: a bulging cornice capping a parallelepiped and two semi-cylinders, a huge bay window equivalent to the double-height of the living room and a vast white rectangle framed by bricks hanging over the entrance. They will provide a disquieting twist to the classical arrangement and evoke "the architectural drama."

In 1923, Le Corbusier mentioned how impressed he was by Michelangelo's work in Saint Peter's in Rome. He described the basilica as a magisterial composition of simple volumes, cylinders and prisms. He admires the work of the artist who shaped monumental ornaments to add to the simple base and, in so doing, communicated passion and drama to the whole. Michelangelo is a magnificent first name that went down in history instead of a surname.

*From left to right: Amédée Ozenfant, Albert Jeanneret and Le Corbusier in the villa Jeanneret in La Chaux-de-Fonds.*



Among the ten proposals that Le Corbusier sent to the director of commercial matters at the Banque immobilière parisienne (BIP), in charge of the development on the square du Docteur-Blanche, only the inseparable bodies of the villas La Roche and Jeanneret-Raaf were built, at the back of the dead end. Thus, two supporters of Corbusian architecture were to strike the deal: Albert Jeanneret, his brother, was a musician, and Raoul La Roche, his Swiss friend, was a banker and an art collector. Le Corbusier and Ozenfant introduced La Roche to purist and cubist painting and he supported the ideas of *L'Esprit nouveau* to the point of becoming a shareholder. These clients were friends and relatives.

March 1923-April 1925. The development on the square du Docteur-Blanche demanded that the architects do some patient research and rewriting. The representative of the BIP snuck out of the picture, the clients were hesitant. The project came to a sudden end. Nevertheless, since 1922, Le Corbusier had been multiplying his contacts in order to get a contract for architectural developments, like his Dutch or German colleagues. Because the development in "series" was an answer to the anarchy and the thankless confusion of individual constructions. The principle is void of class distinctions and is equally valid for mass housing as for middle-class villas. The idea is present not only in Lège and Pessac, but also in Vaucresson, around the villa Besnus. The result of a disappointment, the villa La Roche (and its continuation, the villa Jeanneret-Raaf) came out of the ordeal with the status of an example. Closely following the wishes and views of a learned man, the "architectural promenade" was at its peak here: the main part of the house was intended to be the route to the art gallery. Raoul La Roche was a bachelor: the living quarters were relegated to the second floor. Only the dining room was on the first floor.

On the white walls of the villa hang Picasso, Braque, Juan Gris, Jeanneret and Ozenfant. "We'll go look for painters to blow up the walls that are bothering us," wrote Le Corbusier. For the first time, and in a house devoted to painting, the architect used color *intra muros*; it was rhythmic, dynamic, it accompanied the step and the pause and came in the three ranges defined by Le Corbusier and Ozenfant a couple of years earlier. Polychromy as applied to architecture was in the air. At the core of the new pictorial aesthetics of the Dutch De Stijl group (Piet Mondrian and Theo Van Doesburg), polychromy was also at the centre of discussions between Le Corbusier and Fernand Léger.

# Villa La Roche

**Project architects:** Le Corbusier and Pierre Jeanneret.
**Client:** Raoul La Roche, director of the Crédit commercial de France bank and modern art collector.
**Construction dates:** 1923-1925.
**Description:** Art gallery and studio.
**Location:** 10, square du Docteur-Blanche, in Paris, 16th arrondissement.
**Current condition:** Villa-museum, headquarters of the Fondation Le Corbusier.

The villa La Roche is cause for optimism. It is a reminder that there once was a time in Paris when there were rich and established people who wanted to understand. Today those people are elsewhere.

What did they want to understand? That, in the aftermath of a terrible war, it was possible to view the modern world as a happy adventure. To understand and assume responsibility for this world and, since riches stimulate the appetite, to take advantage of its new developments daily. In a world that needs rebuilding, intense pleasure in the new may be ranked as a moral requirement: the new is radical.

To those who wondered and wanted to experience their time, Le Corbusier wished to offer the opportunity to live in a coherent environment, beyond the mere consumption of goods. According to Le Corbusier, life will recover its meaning, and beauty its character, if art, industry, technique, architecture, urban planning and all the creative forces of society overcome their contradictions and come together around a set of rational values: clarity, exactness, precision, performance and so forth.

This is the modern project. In order to bring it about, Corbusian thinking must skirt the shadow of a war in which engineers and industrialists went astray – the same engineers and industrialists who supplied him with an irreproachably poetic material. These heroes of the rational world got lost because war itself is deeply irrational. Their basic energy was warped because it was not guided by a more elevated way of thinking. The spiritual trend capable of getting them back on track was to be led by art – a "purist" art, a total art form that would transcend reality as a whole.



***Opposite page:*** **North facade seen from the first floor landing.**

The modern individual who appreciates planes, boats and mechanics is also in love with peace. To keep him from straying once again into a world of violence, art will signpost his environment. The villa La Roche is a complete work that serves as a *vade-mecum* and is informative about all aspects of modernity. In its complexity, the villa represents what a modern city could be. At the same time it is a place to live, a sculpture, a painting, a piece of furniture, an item of clothing. It is also a theater, picturesque because it is demonstrative: the double height of the entrance with its boxes and balconies makes for a suitable stage. The villa is full of surprises and new developments: it mixes interior with exterior, natural with man-made, emptiness with densely filled space, white with bright colors, and art with industry.

Its architecture does not let go of the man it is trying to convince and transform. It is constantly making demands on that person. To draw him inside, the architecture reveals its depths by increasing the slant

perspectives and transparencies. It leads him along its seams and holds him close to its ceilings after having led him through impressive spaces. In every way, it seeks to keep him awake as if to ward off a nightmare; its grip increases as he gets closer to the private rooms. The architecture goes so far as to fill these rooms with color, nooks, crannies and events – places where, if left alone, the occupant risks dozing off. Having accompanied the body of its patrons so closely, the villa La Roche remains to this day a work where their presence lives on. Its touching quality helps it steer clear of the threat of didacticism.

Le Corbusier is everywhere. Like an artist in his studio, we see him working with the crudest materials and understand his ambition – to fuse the elements of the industrial world with his approach to the visual arts, diverting and transforming them, and work on the convergence of art and reality.

For example, he takes a piece of twisted wire-netting, shapes it into a design and displays it framed. He turns industrial windows into transparent paintings that he hangs on the white walls of the facades. He places a light bulb, a simple light bulb, at the end of a horizontal tube and makes it into a sculpture. He turns a rubber floor into a pink monochrome. The monochrome walls are organized to form a three-dimensional colored composition. A sheet-metal door found in a catalog is promoted to the rank of front door. The hall is lit with the cathedral glass used in factories.

Everything is simple, everything fits into the world order. The radically new beauty of the villa becomes accessible. It seems like something you might have thought up yourself. In the same way, some people think that modern paintings could have been produced by a child.

The mind understands, it wants to participate and the educated eye takes a fresh look at the trivialities of the modern world. These become so many possibilities for comfort, open to our fantasies and made for action.

The new world is an adventure. The villa La Roche is its training ground.

**North facade and villa Jeanneret.**
**North facade seen from the first floor.**

***Opposite page:* Eastern facade.**

LE CORBUSIER
A PARIS
LE CORBUSIER
OEUVRE TISSE

*Opposite page:* Stairway and balcony overlooking the entrance.

*Following pages:* View of the living room with ramp.

Living room and ramp seen from the mezzanine.

North facade and living room.

# Cité de Lège

**Project architects:** Le Corbusier and Pierre Jeanneret.

**Client:** Henry Frugès (1879-1974), industrialist from Bordeaux, France.

**Construction dates:** 1923-1925.

**Description:** Development for factory workers: seven family homes and one collective house for single men (including a canteen and accommodation).

**Location:** Lège, Gironde, France.

**Current condition:** The houses were restored in 1996-1998 by architect Jean-Luc Veyret.

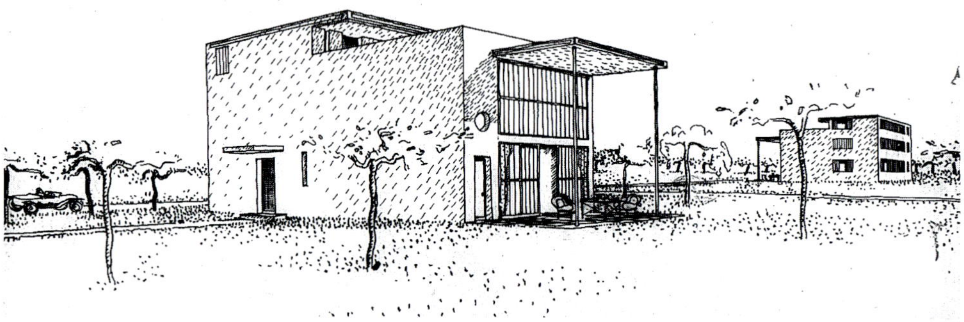

In November 1923, the Bordeaux industrialist Henry Frugès contacted Le Corbusier about a project for a small housing development for workers close to one of his factories, a sawmill in the Landes region. Le Corbusier had just finished a book entitled *Vers une architecture,* a collection of a dozen essays published in *L'Esprit nouveau* (an arts magazine that he had founded in 1920 with the painter Amédée Ozenfant). The book was a great success. Henry Frugès read it and immediately became an energetic supporter of Le Corbusier and his "ideas on logic and progress."
As the heir of a theoretical study researched by Le Corbusier during the war and haunted by the issues of reconstruction, the workers' development in Lège was part of a vast outpouring of mass-produced and minimal housing projects to which Le Corbusier had devoted himself since 1914. Le Corbusier had read Albert de Foville's *Enquête sur les conditions de l'habitation en France* (1894) and had gathered information on the new architecture of the British suburbs. He was outraged by the French "crisis" and was increasing his attempts to get into the market of workers' housing. Henry Frugès gave him his first break with a prototype called the "maison du Tonkin" in the center of Bordeaux (it was destroyed in 1975). For Lège, Frugès bought an Ingersoll-Rand cement gun. On the site, Le Corbusier set off to master liberating industrial techniques: cement sprayed onto a dismountable box, minimal surfaces, roof terraces and so forth. Lège looked to the future. Lège went too fast. The incompetency of the design office and the architect's unfamiliarity with sprayed cement jeopardized the success of the building. These problems would come up again in Pessac.



# Modern district, Frugès

**Project architects:** Le Corbusier and Pierre Jeanneret.

**Client:** Henry Frugès.

**Construction dates:** 1924-1926.

**Description:** Garden city of about fifty houses (the initial plan of July 1924 was for 135).

**Location:** Pessac, Gironde, France.

**Current condition:** Rehabilitation in progress. One house bought by the city is used for a museum.

In 1924, Henri Frugès – entrepreneur in the sugar industry and art collector – bought a field in the Landes region in order to build a garden-city "in the pure air of the pine forest" for the homeless and prolong the Lège experience. At a moment when France was going through a serious social housing crisis, the industrialist fulfilled his civic duty. He also wanted to break even on his investment in equipment bought for the Lège site (Ingersoll-Rand cement gun, compressors, grinders, mixers).
For Le Corbusier, Pessac was a stroke of luck. It was the ideal place to develop on a large scale an appropriate answer to the issues of mass housing and workers' accommodation. In 1924, the residential program included 135 houses with shops in the middle of the complex. There were four models offered: houses with arches, "skyscraper," in alternate rows, or detached with a roof terrace. In 1925, Pierre Jeanneret added an entrance: a standard six-story portico apartment building with roof terraces (*immeuble-portique*).
During construction, the technical and financial difficulties piled up, slowing down and weakening the experience: construction was taken over by a Parisian entrepreneur, the cement-gun was replaced by breeze-blocks, the dimensions were not precise, there were construction defects. The excess costs soared wildly. In 1926, when 51 houses were finally delivered, there was no water! It was a case of sheer neglect. Frugès and Le Corbusier had a

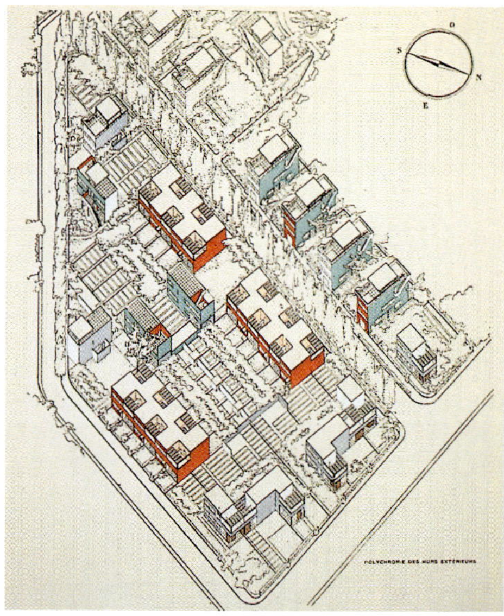

temporary building permit (which was not extended) and they showed absolutely no concern for the most elementary rules of collective living. The houses would not be sold until 1928 because of the Loucheur law. Neither Jeanneret's portico building nor the shops were ever built.

# Lège and Pessac

Opening ceremony, Pessac, May 1926.

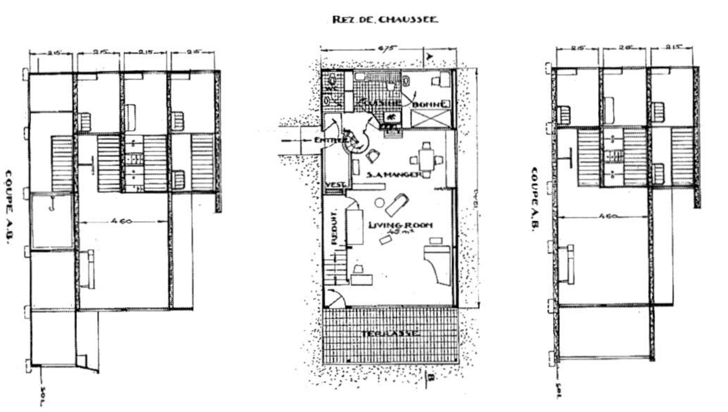


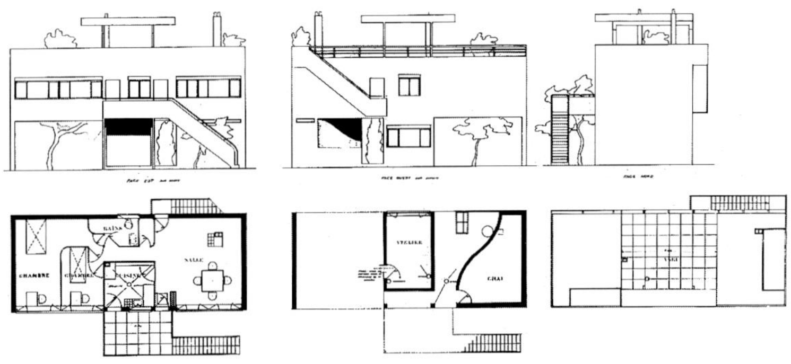

Lège.
Old
communal
house
and
pelota
fronton.

Lège. Northern view of houses.

# Here, the buildings have no secrets.

They are naked and show off their assets. There are no tricks. Nothing but the truth, Le Corbusier always boasted.

On the basis of the housing projects in Lège and Pessac, one is inclined to believe him and share his contempt for style, decoration and other misleading devices: they are cheats. What a shame.

The suburban houses sprouting there should be ashamed of displaying their taste for the picturesque and the fake. But they are shrewd. They seem to be saying, "Haven't your modern constructions – so simple, so self-confident – drawn their inspiration from white cubical buildings in Greece, Algeria or Morocco? Don't they in turn obey a style, an exotic one at that?"

Such a response is not entirely incorrect. Refraining from lying is not the same as telling the truth, just as stripping down to bare essentials is not sufficient proof that there has been no cheating. In order to be right, it is necessary to put forward an argument. Le Corbusier did not lack for arguments. First, he intended to use modern production techniques to build these houses: standardization, mass production, reinforced concrete, "cement-guns" and so on. These techniques were supposed to facilitate low-cost building and provide superior living conditions: more available space, free floorspace, roof terraces, loggias, pergolas, and so on. Secondly, he thought that the Frugès employees formed a working community with a spirit that should be evident in the organization of their housing development. Collective landmarks were necessary. Such landmarks would convey far stronger feelings than the usual sentiment of "each to his own" represented by individual houses with their fake style. These landmarks are provided for by modern aesthetics. Drawing inspiration from the world of machines, with an unbiased outlook on the world, modern aesthetics would appeal to the workers directly in a way they would naturally learn to appreciate.

In order to begin to be understood, Le Corbusier removed the formulas commonly used to describe houses from his language. A typical comment is: a Basque-style house with a tile roof, a wood-framed entrance, foundation of inlaid stone and windows framed in brick. Le Corbusier describes Pessac as a Zigzag house, houses in alternate rows and, further on, a detached house, "skyscraper" and twin houses.

The abstract picture of the development acts as a substitute for the genre painting of individual villas. Type replaces style. But type, because of its variations, here constitutes an open system. It offers real possibilities to choose between interior and exterior spaces that correspond to quite real assets.

This set of buildings sets the mind at ease. The result of the coupling

Lège.
Old
communal
house and
house.

Lège.
Southwestern
view of
houses.

Pessac.
"Skyscraper"
buildings
seen from the
street.

Pessac.
House with
terrace
(foreground).

of a basic module and a very simple aesthetic, the project evokes the directions printed on the boxes of children's building sets: simple constructions of modular pieces piled up or fitted together. These games have simple rules and do not allow cheating. They enable the building of elementary, reassuring worlds. Witness the houses of Lège: cubes whose simplicity is touching in its evocation of the humble and dignified lives of workers. Witness the houses of Pessac: successful variations of individual units sheltering a small community that, having mastered its environment, knows where it is heading.

These housing projects satisfy those who dream of neutral living conditions, of a shell they can fill themselves. This simplicity does not boil down to a style – "purism" in this case; it is not simply a branch of aesthetics. Neutrality is a trait of the modern world which guarantees a certain degree of liberty. It is independent of traditional hierarchies and is well suited to the individual who would like to design his own environment. It allows its inhabitants to find their bearings. Although the neutrality of the architecture involves the rejection of any decorative touches, when its inhabitant chooses to bare himself, he does it less out of aesthetic concern or aloofness than out of conviction. The projects in Lège and Pessac evoke the *kibbutzim*, immigrant constructions, the rough dwellings of those who, having turned their backs on the past, envisaged their futures while rolling up their sleeves. The reigning atmosphere is favorable to action and commitment. The idea that his workers were committed to architectural activism no doubt pleased M. Frugès.

One accepts this reconsideration of community housing projects without reservations. However, a disturbing impression remains. One has the sensation of being on a set. Whereas the quality of the whole, including its aesthetic value, lies in the neutrality of its different parts, the polychromy of the buildings niggles. It is reminiscent of the traditional hierarchized world where the architect occupies a pre-eminent position, emphasizing the gestures he makes to produce the beautiful. The polychromy is an added aesthetic value that weighs heavily. Of course, it is inspired by the best of the era, but, by turning the project into a vast pictural composition, it transforms a set of simple houses stripped of ornamentation into a scheme for directing collective life. In brief, the project affirms that modern art is a kind of daily hygiene. To expect the people living there to conform to it would be to impose upon their convictions. Stripped of their old rags, they had to put on this motley attire to celebrate the "synthesis of the arts." Polychromy indoctrinates. It must have been the era.

In terms of housing developments our era has nothing to teach.

**Pessac. Western facade and garden.**

Pessac. "Skyscraper" and house with terrace.

Reproducing Lège or Pessac today would be considered far too radical and unprofitable. It is so simple, however, and requires so little foresight and so little courage

*Opposite page:* Pessac. Row house.

23

On August 5, 1923, Mr. Jeanneret wrote in his diary: "Our son Edouard is proposing that we build a tiny little 'purist' house. Our financial means: 3,000 F income in all, it's extraordinarily little." By Christmas 1925, the retirement villa was completed on the bank of Lake Geneva, facing the Alps. Here, the old artisan watch face enameler, who had come down from the Fond valley and its stern Neuchâtel mountains for the mild climate of the lake and the vineyards. Those were full and exuberant years. Le Corbusier was 36 years old and working with Pierre Jeanneret on studio-residences for the painter Ozenfant, the sculptors Lipchitz and Miestchaninoff, and the Terniesens. The year 1923 was also devoted to the development on square du Docteur-Blanche in Paris. The negotiations with the Banque immobilière parisienne on the subject of the square were tough and did not lead anywhere. However, the first arguments with the painter and future neighbor, Gaston Vaudou, in Corseaux, proved fruitful and facilitated a simple, luminous project.

In the beginning, Le Corbusier had imagined a Swiss chalet. Then it was a two-story house. In 1924, he established the definite plan: a "box lying on the ground" of about sixty square meters (4 meters deep by 16 meters long and 2.5 meters high). It also included a single window 11 meters long and a roof terrace.

As a contemporary of the strip-windows in the villas La Roche and Jeanneret, "playing a leading part in the house," the window in Corseaux is exceptional because of the view it frames. The landscape is omnipresent and even more so from the roof terrace Le Corbusier imagined as pastoral: covered with wild geraniums or forget-me-nots sown by the wind.

Over the years some modifications took place. The north facade was covered with galvanized iron shingle and because "houses also catch whooping cough," a hinge was built on the terrace and the south facade was covered with aluminum cladding.

A small book written by Le Corbusier and published in Zurich in 1954, tells the story of the little house (*Une petite maison*), that a haughty council deemed "a crime against nature" and forbid that it ever be imitated.

The architect's mother lived there until she died in 1960.



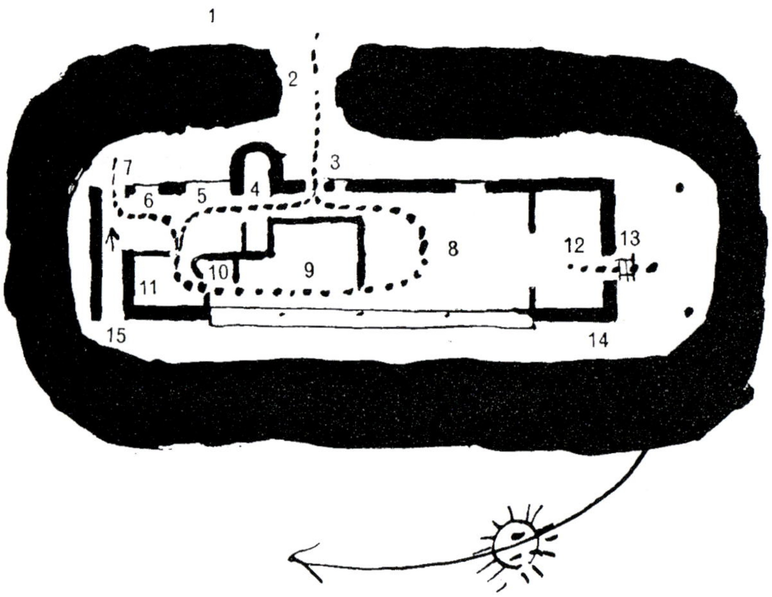

# La petite maison

**Project architect:** Le Corbusier.
**Construction dates:** 1923-1924
**Description:** Retirement house for Mr. and Mrs. Jeanneret.
**Location:** 21, route de Lavaux, Corseaux near Vevey, Switzerland.
**Current condition:** Classified, since June 22, 1962, as a historical monument by the municipal authorities of the canton de Vaud.

Strip window seen from the inside.

*Opposite page:* View of exterior and lake.

# Doing the minimum does not mean being lazy; living with the minimum does not imply destitution.

In order to understand minimal living conditions, it is necessary to take a serious look at how goods are consumed. Precisely what pleasures can be expected from buildings? And, in more general terms – since it is the organization of life that we are dealing with – exactly what is needed? The minimum demands precision. Driven by economy, it filters desires and needs, retaining only the essentials.

The minimum is the first measure of our desires. If it satisfies only a few of our desires, in return it expresses them frankly and makes the things its establishes easily desirable. The desire to live in the little house in Corseaux is immediate. There, we recognize the precise geography of the dreams of a life that could be our own.

If an architect seeks the minimal form, he is limited to defining the expected benefits precisely.

Consider a window. Essentially, it offers views of the scenery and lets in light. The minimal window has no shape until the desired views are defined and the effects of the light imagined. In Corseaux, the panorama of the Alps beyond the lake should be visible from either a standing or a sitting position. A single window can do the job. Eleven meters long, set at the right height, it allows the view of the mountain range to unroll without interruption. The minimum may be large, but it is never oversized. Does one want to enjoy the morning sun, gently, without waking up blinded? The roof rises on the east side and a sky-light is arranged so that the light is diffused on the ceiling and the walls – easy on the eyes. Is a reference opening required in the laundry-room? A glass block fitted in the roof will do.

Consider the roof. It is made to top the construction and protect against bad weather. In Corseaux, the idea is to take advantage of its high elevation and, as no attic is needed, the roof is flat. One can walk onto it to enjoy an exceptional view. Furthermore, since no land was to be wasted, the roof is a garden. There was also a need for sheltered porch: the roof extends beyond the east gable and there it is, a shed. One can dream big and think minimally. There is leeway. The minimum exhausts things by using them several times, moving them or piling them up.

The roof terrace serves as a garden and covers an outdoor shed which is protected by a sliding partition when necessary. The window is lined lengthwise by an interior window-sill used for displaying trinkets and fitted with a sink; a folding table which seats four to six people is fixed to it. A hidden partition slides to close off a room while simultaneously offering closet space. In one bedroom, there are

**East gable.**



bunkbeds and a low piece of furniture for storage serves as a platform for a chair and a fixed desk: an office in the air. In the guest bedroom, a spare bed on wheels can be pulled out of the floor from under the bed. A small door, set flush in the opposite wall, provides access to a built-in sink; on the back of the door are a mirror and a towel rack: a concealable wash-stand. Lighting fixtures are articulated to light up different spots. The bedroom and bathroom are open to enlarge the perception of space. The pipes running between the radiators ensure efficient heating.

Profit is sought in every detail; the stakes are doubled.

But is this frenzied quest for profitability and efficiency not the sign of a narrow mind? Because these elements are not attractive in themselves. A sink, an articulated metal lamp, a bed made of steel tubes, the skinny prop that supports the shed – Le Corbusier mockingly called it a "column" – all of these elements make for summary decor. Besides, four meters wide is a bit narrow for a house.

As if by magic, however, the combination of these humble elements makes for a little house that is both charming and profound.

In order to appreciate the house, it is necessary simply to enjoy Le Corbusier's irony when he plays at diverting objects from their initial function and highlights them. The sink set in its niche, its white curves reflected in the mirror, is an acceptable icon for those who are willing to play the game. The sliding partition becomes a noble event. The accessible roof resembles the deck of a ship drifting on the lake. The bunkbeds prolong the simple period of childhood. In short, there is sleight of hand at work in Corseaux. Using bits and pieces and sliding folding screens, Le Corbusier makes a pretty bird appear. It is charming, delightful, and shows no sign of pretension. It is so light it becomes profound. The small house is a model of a discreet human dwelling. It can be used as an example by the industrial and urban civilization which fills a frightening amount of space and runs the risk of weighing down the planet to the point of exhaustion.

This is a constantly changing civilization: it imposes perpetual motion on those wanting to capture its spirit. The little house in Corseaux will accompany these shifts while remaining the least cumbersome possible. For instance, it was only a blueprint in Le Corbusier's pocket while he looked for a suitable piece of land. Planned according to specific wishes, it is detached from any ground or tradition to which it may be rooted. The house is here, it could have been anywhere. It would simply have been necessary to look further afield for a piece of land corresponding to its purpose. This is architecture turned upside down. The dominant architectural culture worries about this type of detachment.

It appreciates houses that are rooted in the landscape. It teaches us that the eye judges a building based on the knowledge of the examples singled out for distinction by history or convention. It illustrates the fact that architecture is the art of citing and arranging styles. It seeks to seduce by the prettiness of its language whose references are deemed to be definitive and known to all.

The little house in Corseaux is break-and-enter architecture. Situated outside of the ordinary limits of the discipline, it does not employ traditional methods of seduction. Le Corbusier sees these as cunning commonplaces void of meaning. In order to be attractive, the little house uses arguments built from scratch. They are convincing in so much as the people who were to live in the little house were attracted *a priori*: they were the architect's parents.

**Planted roof.**

**Living room corner.**

Cross view.

Living room with pictures of Le Corbusier and his mother.

Dining room.

*Opposite page:* Window opening onto the lake.

*Le Corbusier and Mies Van der Rohe at Weissenhof (1927).*

"However important its technical and economical aspects may be, the problem of modern housing is, first and foremost, a problem of architecture." That is how, in 1927, Mies Van der Rohe began the experimental development of Weissenhof in Stuttgart where he was chief architect.
Mies was responsible for the block layout and gave his guests carte blanche. They were among the most active modern European architects in Rotterdam, Berlin and Dessau. Le Corbusier was charmed and flattered. In 1926, the inauguration of the workers' housing development in Pessac, near Bordeaux, had brought an end to wonderful, but exhausting work. Weissenhof appeared to be a pleasant contract in a context of theoretical and fraternal competition.
While Mies Van der Rohe proposed to work on the flexibility of the plan by erecting a little metal-framed building, and Walter Gropius sought to facilitate prefabrication of detached houses, Le Corbusier constructed his "Citrohan" model house. The plans had been in his files since the 1922 Salon d'automne. This complete prototype of the "machine for living," freed from the floor and the site, which could be transplanted anywhere, in a city or on the seashore, widely discussed and dreamed about by the architect, found, on the side of a hill overlooking Stuttgart, the opportunity of being built. It was at Weissenhof that Le Corbusier formulated the "Five Points for a New Architecture," published in the ninth issue of the magazine *Die Form*: 1, the *pilotis*; 2, the open plan; 3, the strip window; 4, the open facade; 5, the roof terrace.

# Houses at Weissenhof

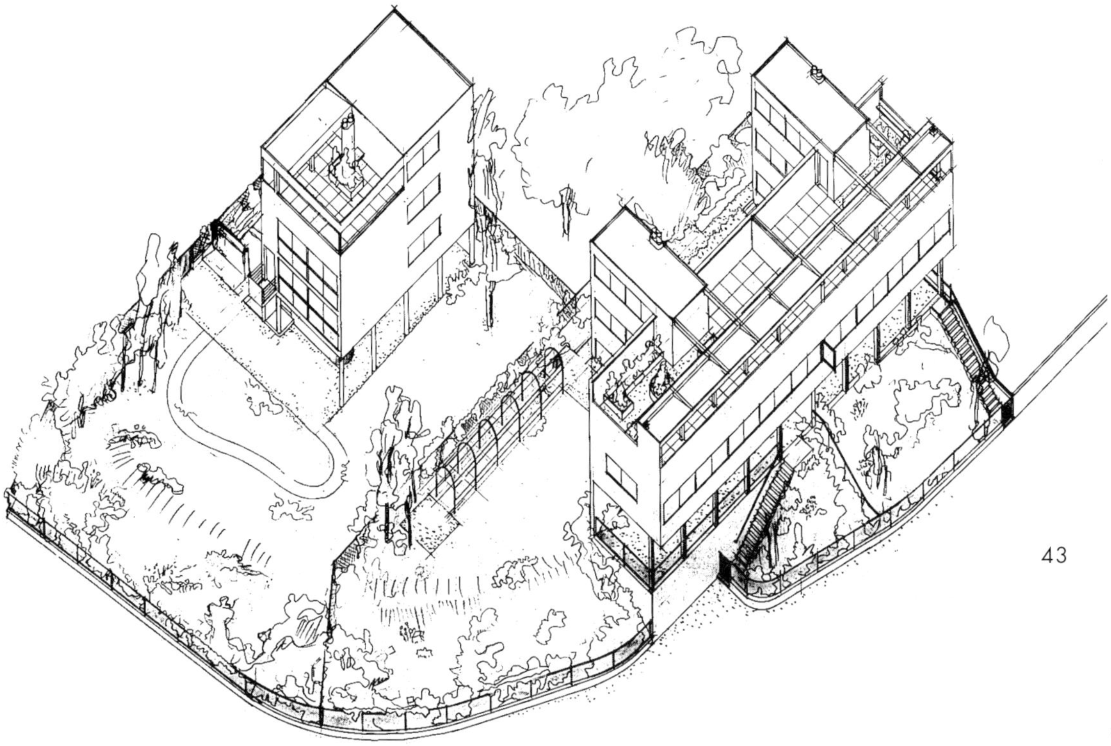



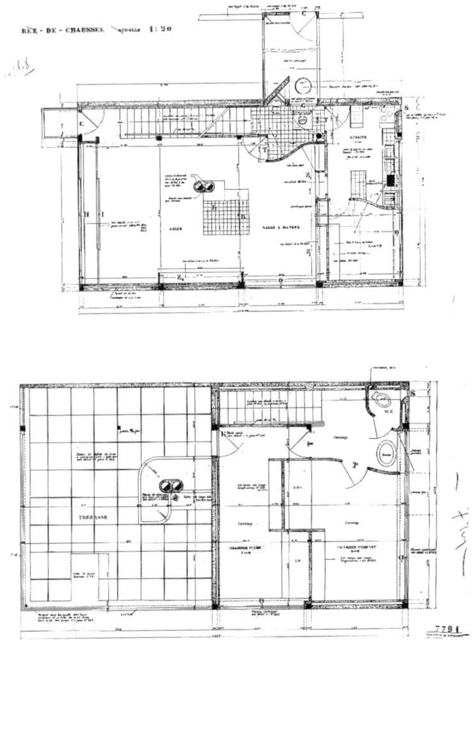

**Invited architects:** Victor Bourgeois (Brussels), Le Corbusier and Pierre Jeanneret (Paris), J.J.P. Oud and Mart Stam (Rotterdam), Josef Frank (Vienna). And the Germans Walter Gropius (Dessau), Peter Behrens, Hans Poelzig, Bruno and Max Taut, Ludwig Hilberseimer, Mies Van der Rohe (Berlin), Adolf Rading, Hans Scharoun (Breslau), Richard Döcker and Adolf Schneck (Stuttgart).

**Developers:** Deutscher Werkbund Association (DWB), vice-president Mies Van der Rohe. He coordinated the Weissenhof project.

**Construction date:** 1927.

**Description of the project:** Design of an experimental development, including individual houses and collective buildings. Le Corbusier puts his name to two individual houses; the larger one comprises two separate dwellings.

**Location:** The outskirts of Stuttgart. The Le Corbusier houses are at 2, Bruckmannweg and 1-3, Tathenaustrasse.

**Current condition:** Partly damaged by bombings between 1942 and 1944, the development was classified as a historical site in 1956, repainted in 1968, then restored and rehabilitated (1981-1986).

House for two families.

*Opposite page:* Single family house.

An essential part of the motor of history has set itself in motion, a new power has come forth: the masses. They turned war into world war, they revolutionized the largest of countries, they worked on assembly lines in order to mass-produce and were active consumers. They moved around and sought entertainment in groups, doing so in ever larger urban centers.

Violence, production and consumerism were no longer conceivable except on a grand scale. Since the scale was large, violence, production and consumerism became the new components of society. Siegfried Giedion was to write that "mechanization takes command." As for Le Corbusier, he quoted Henry Ford whose automobile factories were mass-producing the famous model T that would make speed available to every American.

Repetition, series, the breaking down of ancient equilibriums, social dynamics, fascination with performance and seduction by technology are subjects chosen as starting points by modern architects in order to synchronize the built environment to the changes in society.

Today, a visitor to Weissenhof experiences difficulty in reconciling such ambitions with architecture that seems simply hewn from large white masses and unremarkably functional. The buildings certainly satisfy the essential needs and are rationally constructed, but this is quite a small thing. It is difficult to understand what singles them out besides their rejection of styles from the past.

In fact, since the world finds strength in numbers, it concentrates its energy on satisfying common aspirations to the detriment of the distinctions and hierarchies established by history or tradition. Taken into this movement, modern architecture includes a certain amount of generality. Its scale is global: it is defined outside of historical, social and national factors. Thus, this architecture seems neutral, bare and abstract.

But its detachment is not a loss. It is a radical means of action whose goal is less moral – by the value it gives to renunciation – than political. Modern architecture has a program that is defined by three points.

First, it erases social differences and promises to be accessible to everyone. Le Corbusier used the same vocabulary whether he was building for a captain of industry or his employee: stripped down space, painted concrete, steel fixtures, furniture made of metal tubing and so on. He thought that a modest house and a palace were comparable: it was a question of worthiness. Access to this quality is not costly: dignity comes from the harmony of the lines and the intelligence of the arrangements. On the other hand, decoration is considered a false dream and a social aberration because it tampers with the purity of line, rewards the individual who can adorn himself with it and

denigrates the individual who is satisfied with cheap imitations.

Second, modern architecture is international. Drawing inspiration from the changes occurring along lines common to all of the industrialized countries, it is intended to be applied identically everywhere, unconcerned with context or customs. Although the architects who built at Weissenhof came from different countries – Germany, Holland, Belgium, and France – their buildings constitute a common culture and both their appearance and their spirit are similar. An international movement was forming. It was very astonishing. Before then, at international fairs, countries invariably sought to distinguish themselves through their national forms of architecture.

Thirdly, modern architecture largely ignores geographical distinctions and does not hold historical examples in any higher esteem. Modern architecture prefers to forge its own convictions: it plays a part in the course of history, at the avant-garde. It is inspired by the present, up to the point of believing that logical deductions can be drawn from it, by using clearly established observations. It bestows upon the present the same objective virtues as upon science. The only prerequisite is knowing how to observe it.

Therefore, modern architecture is not a new style that depends on trends. On the contrary, it puts an end to "the battle of the styles" by claiming, once and for all, the realms of the present, reason and truth. It introduces a "new spirit" which inspires the human race by the exactness of its concepts, instead of seducing individuals by prettiness of style or impressing them with historical references. Its bareness is displayed with a sense of relief. It is the garment that is best suited to represent its spirit. Modern architecture propagates an egalitarian, universal and progressive ideology.

Today, these manifestos appear to be either sublime or vain, premonitory or naive, essential or transient. It depends.

Modernism was successful because it removed architecture from the closed domain of the academy by supplying it with an imperative which still holds good: lucidity concerning its era. Architecture thus introduced the key to its own renewal. On the other hand, this intelligence shuts the door of the paradise of ready-made history. The "spirit" it quotes as its authority forbids it, in theory, to be frozen in the rules it has formulated. Architecture capsized under the blow of this double change in perspective. Endlessly forced to adapt itself, architecture will be constantly off balance in the future. It invents a destiny for itself which drives it to be intelligent, radical and curious, and evolve at the risk of being incomprehensible.

One should not dwell on the dogmatic character or the schematic

**Northern facade of single family house.**

aspect of the statements made by modern architects. Their emphasis relates to the number of generalities they have chosen to take on, in the manner of an era engaged in a forced march towards uniformity and not lacking in global theories. Therefore, modern architecture is above all a process, a movement in the literal sense of the word. As a result of this stirring effect, it produces its own refutations and, as it is more "spirit" than dogma, it implies future contradictions.
Moreover, conceived and then maintained in a state of emergency, modern architecture constitutes an eschatology. Drawn into the heart of worldwide movements which upset social, national and economic organizations, our civilization runs the risk of losing control. Faced with this situation, a disoriented society cannot neglect the resources of modern architecture which are an essential demonstration of the mind, striking proof of the human capacity for organization, and an expression of a higher culture that cuts across national boundaries. Should society reject these means, modern architects predict that it will be in danger of social upheaval, economic crisis and war. History will unfold according to their predictions without the causes having anything to do with their preoccupations.
Subsequently, some find the paradox of a modern architecture amusing – intended to establish common taste, failing to please the masses, whose tastes ran to trends, decoration, lightness and fakeness, showing little concern for the devaluation of values and styles. This disillusioned point of view, boasting of its own common sense, was rather widespread. Today, we are justly dubious of an architecture that would flaunt moral and political aims based on the way industrial production is organized. There is no doubt that, over the last few years, architecture has not played the role that modern architects wanted to assign to it. It prefers to refer to individual expression, fears to take an advance position on political issues, constitutes a culture that is less clearly defined and, lacking confidence in its ability to enlighten the world, is tempted to entertain it, and takes on social issues without claiming to change society, preferring to soothe the "world's ills." The time has come for modesty, compassion and play. As a consequence, some of the generalities society is seeking to produce in order to ward off the world's constant upheavals do not fall to architecture except as a meagre portion; these are now produced by the entertainment industry which is partial to architectural scenery.
Visitors swarmed to Weissenhof, but did not find a set there. At Weissenhof, modern architecture had its first opportunity to confront the public on the scale of a neighborhood. It sought to convince the masses by way of an ordinary architecture: effective, economical, and neutral.

**Entrance detail.**

**Entrance stairway.**

**View on garden and ground floor.**

48

***Opposite page:*** **House for two families: terrace and entrance.**

The public was both shocked and interested. Weissenhof is still a nice place to live. There, the ordinary conditions of urban life have changed radically, but smoothly. These changes are expressed differently from one building to the next and what is considered ordinary changes according to the architect.
Mies Van der Rohe designed a four-story apartment building and kept everything strictly functional. He seized collective housing without much fondness for the subject and without tempering any of the vagueness involved. Dignity was forced upon ordinary housing by the accuracy of the arrangements, the austerity of the lines and the economy of the design.
On the contrary, J.J.P. Oud, with his experience of Dutch social housing, wanted to offer richer possibilities. His little two-story houses with their modest gardens and small individual courtyards were presented in series. They conveyed an image of an ordinarily happy society, which cultivated ordinary happiness without excess. Here, the individual – as a moderate social being – found dignity and was enriched by the repetition of daily tasks.
Le Corbusier was also interested in everyday life. However, when he carefully arranged all the details of home life, it was in order to do a better job of shaking up the resident. Le Corbusier roused him and made him adopt gestures and postures that opened him up to the promise of adventure brought by each new day. For Le Corbusier, the individual comes first and lives in a daily state of exaltation. The individual does not disappear behind an abstract drawing, does not dissolve in a group, does not rely on collective representation. He is an actor and he needs a set. Not a decorated one as that would be an affectation – decorum rather, which watches over the unfolding of everyday life and offers the inhabitant a mixture of real assets and constraints so that his life will always seem more noble and extraordinary.
A house is a palace, it is a question of dignity according to Le Corbusier. When the palace becomes a home, it must not cast aside its greatness. Le Corbusier's concern about enlarging man's gestures can be found in each of the "five points for a new architecture." His buildings at Weissenhof were the first to very literally illustrate these five points.
The *pilotis* place the house in the air and its inhabitant in an overhanging position. The ground floor plays second fiddle, it has no access to the garden: it doesn't encourage making use of the soil or the triviality of gardening.
The roof garden *(toit-jardin)* is a favorite spot. Vegetation will grow there if allowed to do so and when it does, it does so because of human ingenuity rather than natural means. Up on the roof garden, one is closer

to the sky and to exercising one's will than to the earth and submitting to nature's whims. The walled terrace protects against the elements: space is contained in a kind of open room, but one nevertheless feels an infinite amount of freedom. The garden lower down seems a bit meagre and, if there are vegetables planted there, the garden evokes subsistence.
The open plan *(plan libre)* ignores the restraint of load-bearing walls. On the second floor, the partition walls can slide like closet doors to turn three minimal bedrooms and a small living room into a large open space. Everything there is confused at the cost of intimacy and for the benefit of size and perspective. Le Corbusier explained that the apartment's design was inspired by a sleeping-car. Minimal housing and everyday life profit from the performance of modernity: everything moves and one can claim to be here – in one's own individual cell – and elsewhere at once as part of a large communal space. The only requirement is enjoyment of the trip.
The strip window *(fenêtre en longueur)* reinterprets, horizontally in rooms with low ceilings, the luxury of high windows in seventeenth-century mansions. The individual, having grown taller, leans out and enjoys a panorama. The outside is fully given over to him; he gathers information there and the world calls out to him.
The open facade *(façade libre)* offers the architect a plane where he can provide windows as long, as fine and as high as he thinks necessary to express "the drama of architecture."
With Le Corbusier everything was big, but he was not motivated by vanity. This excessiveness suited him when he wished to accompany the world's vast movements and adopt their rhythms. If he expected to influence that course and accompany progress on its march, he had to bid higher, for fear that the movement of the world, backfiring, might make the machine run backwards.
He believed that mankind, when presented with greatness, would not regress.

**House for two families: southern facade and separation between units.**



***Opposite page:*** **Single family house, detail of the northern facade.**

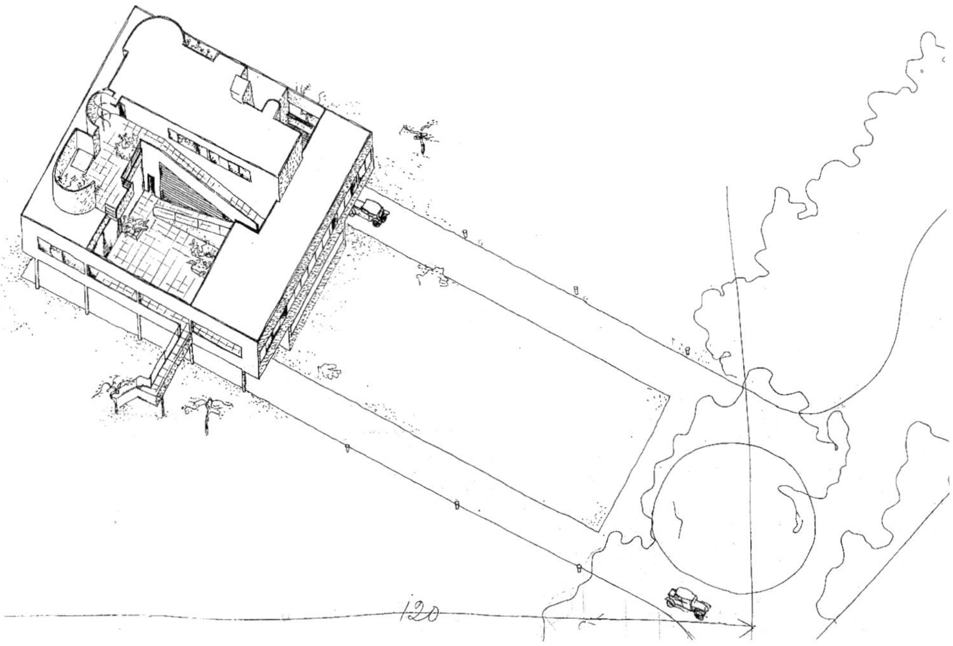


In 1928, Mr. and Mrs. Pierre Savoye, frequent guests at the villa Church in Ville-d'Avray, hired Le Corbusier to design a weekend house a few kilometers outside of Paris. The ground on which the house was to be built was a meadow on top of a hill, free of any constraint, ideal for planting a "box in the air" overlooking the Seine river.
The villa Savoye was based on that gamble on freedom. It was a contract asking for air and light that was landed by a disorientated man. Le Corbusier had indeed seduced the European avant-garde at Weissenhof in 1927, but, the following year, he was brutally excluded from the competition for the League of Nations building. There was intrigue, scandal and bitterness. He immediately published *Une maison, un palais*. Thus, the villa Savoye was to be perfect. As a strict illustration of the five points of the architectural manifesto laid out in Stuttgart – *pilotis*, free plan, strip-window, open facade and roof terrace – the house that would be named "Les Heures claires" (The Light Hours), claimed high and loud the principles of "circulation," the "promenade," and "architectural freedom" inaugurated in Auteuil with the villa La Roche.
Under the box, passing between the *pilotis*, comes a driveway: another stroke of boldness. The principle of freed space at the level of the *pilotis* allows cars to be driven under the house. It is also a result: already, the second version of the maison Citrohan shown at the 1922 Salon d'automne was presented as partially standing on *pilotis*, the first step toward freeing the ground. In 1926, the project of villas for the princesse de Polignac in Boulogne and Neuilly involved automobiles. The villa Cook in Boulogne (1926-1927) would be the first villa in which Le Corbusier would dare to hollow out the ground floor (now walled up); he would do the same at the villa Baizeau in Carthage (1929). Hesitant after his initial sketches with an automobile option, he renounced this option for the villa Stein and De Monzie in Vaucresson (1926-1928) in favour of servants quarters.
Another characteristic of the Savoye property is the caretaker's accommodation designed by Le Corbusier and Jeanneret: a miniature house of 35 square meters divided in two bedrooms. This model for minimal housing, "House for a single family," was presented by its inventors at the second Congrès international d'architecture moderne (CIAM) – International Congress of Modern Architecture – held in Frankfurt in 1929.

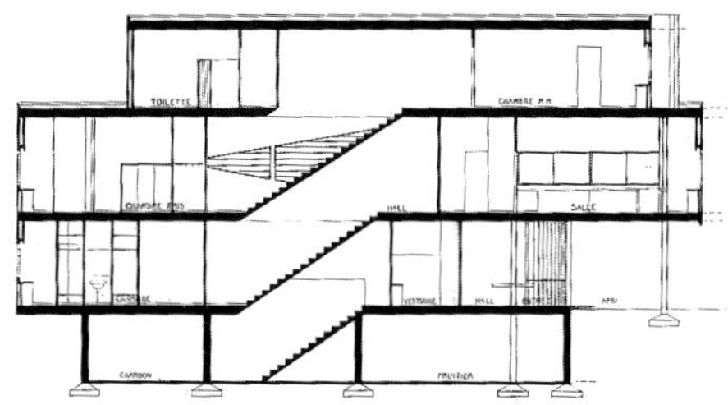

ECHELLE 1:50

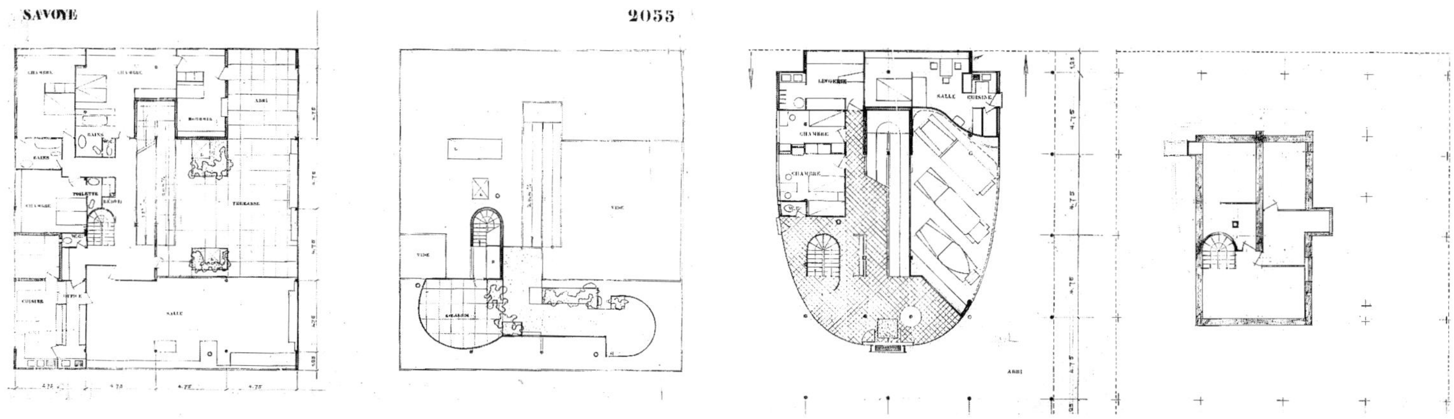

# Villa Savoye

**Project architects:** Le Corbusier and Pierre Jeanneret.
**Clients:** Mr. Pierre Savoye, insurance-broker, and his wife.
**Construction dates:** 1928-1931.
**Description:** Weekend house.
**Location:** Poissy, Yvelines, 25 kilometers from Paris.
**Current condition:** Classified as a historical monument since 1964. Its interior polychromy and garden were restored 1994-1997, under the supervision of Bruno Chauffert-Yvart, Bâtiments de France architect.

# There is no getting used to the villa Savoye.

Even now, it is an irruption. One goes to visit the week-end house of a well-to-do and cultured family and discovers the villa Savoye on a turn in the road: its presence is disturbing. Refusing to mingle with anything surrounding it, it is detached, immaculate and in suspension. One wonders. What does it say of the appetite for life of a wealthy couple who enjoyed entertaining guests? What of the pleasures derived from being rich, cultured and out in the country? How does it set its inhabitants apart?

The villa Savoye hardly even hears these questions. Its influence was established independently of a human presence. Whether empty or occupied, seen or ignored, it conserves its stature. Haughty, it refuses to recycle a single familiar image that would evoke a house or residence – with a share of nostalgia and faded shadows – the emollient for comfort and domesticity. It is lively, snappy, quick-tempered and full of definitive statements. First of all, one admires its aplomb.

Ambitious to the point of wanting to emancipate itself from the heaviness of built things, it moves in the realm of pure thought: vigorous thought lifts up the villa and strives to make nature slide under it. It is less concerned with sparing the greenery than with not mixing with it, owing it nothing. There is no natural extension to the villa and no use of natural materials. The villa is not in a natural setting, it is on the same level as nature. Both nature and the villa simply exist. The first is shaped by the surge of biological forces, the second is produced by the gears of modern forces. There is a lot of pretension. In order to be granted this pre-eminent place in the nature of things, it must prove its persuasiveness.

The villa is obliged to convince. In order to do so, it picks up the arguments developed by Le Corbusier in his writings. They deal with principles. These principles are lofty and the result of an enthusiastic reading of modernity: life principles as applied to the modern individual, aesthetical and constructive principles, general principles composed of truths. These firm intentions apply directly to the villa which constitutes a suitable device for organizing life's little details.

The experience of living in the villa should thus be formative. It is this that singles out its residents: they bring life to a beacon and are perfectly aware of doing so. This adherence could dissolve into doubt – it is not always comfortable to lend one's own flesh to the modern cause – and one could lose track of Le Corbusier's arguments. In order to avoid this situation, he organized a ceremonial. By manipulating bodies (ours), his protocol sought to reorientate our minds according to the polarities induced by the "live sources of modern matter." The displacements – "the architectural promenade" – are such that sensory experience

**Villa in its natural surroundings.**

***Opposite page:*** **Ground floor and driveway.**

**Living room corner with reflection.**

**Bathroom off the main bedroom.**

interrogates the mind. We must take Le Corbusier literally when he said that he had invented a "machine to inspire emotion."
Thus it is a question of movement and, to have a better go at whisking people along, the villa starts by destabilizing them. Choreography follows.
Stunned by its muteness and dazzled by its whiteness, one imagines the villa to be highly compact, then one realizes that space insinuates itself into it and spreads across it through and through. One.thinks one can understand its effects as they are extremely simple. But the square plan is less intended to facilitate perception than to constitute a pivot at the heart of the entire space whose four sides face the four horizons. Since the sky seems to turn around this pivot, one turns to get to the entrance which does not appear at once. One hopes, cowardly, to discover a traditional sign of domestic civility, but one gets the feeling that the welcome is a secondary issue. The important thing is that, whether walking or driving, one turns.
One passes a curved partition wall made of frosted glass that blurs outlines. The entrance is not wide. To avoid obstructing it, one advances toward a ramp. The ramp is astonishing. It seems to be an essential part of the ceremony. One follows it without having to look down at one's feet, unlike a stairway. It may be climbed with dignity: the head remains clear and the mind also. In a double ascension, body and mind continuously ascend the light coming from the upper floor: the ramp is a psychopomp. Since it is narrow, it guides visitors one by one, in a procession. One does not engage in conversation during the ascent, one becomes converted.
On the first floor, the terrace is so large, the rooms are so glazed, that it becomes difficult to distinguish between interior and exterior. The light is so generous that one would like to float in it. In order to rest, one lies down on the "grand large" chair. The body fits into its reversed curves in a posture more conducive to thought than to numbness. One may also take a seat in the "grand confort" chair: the trunk is held upright, enabling one to speak clearly.
One gets up to operate the crank that opens the large window overlooking the terrace. The window slides open, one goes out toward a wide, long opening which frames a view of the landscape. One stops there for a moment: nature is calmed. One turns around to follow another ramp leading to the solarium. Up there, a concrete veil, all sensual curves, its frame left bare, is an incitation to take off one's clothes. As close as possibe to the sun, the body regenerates itself. Through a square perforation in the veil, one can confront the city. Further on, in perspective, are work and action. Full of fresh energy and

dressed again, one rushes toward them, spiralling down the staircase that leads back to the entrance. One does not stop in the bedrooms, minimal spaces for simple recuperation. There is so much to do.
Le Corbusier is someone who knew how to stop and think.
He was not tied up by conventions of any kind. The open plan, the open spaces, the box on a *pilotis*, the four strip windows as the only perforations in the facade, the hanging terrace, the flat accessible roof, the sculptural structure on the roof: this is upturned architecture of cheerful casualness. Everything is recombined at the heart of this almost stubbornly simple building.
Le Corbusier took on board the fact that the modern, industrial and mechanistic world levels out old hierarchies and rends past distinctions superfluous. His genius lay in having understood that this world would rise higher if it came to terms with its basic triviality and that this would hold true for the coming century.
Triviality plays a part in all of the villa Savoye's details. It is present in the painted concrete and in the thinness of the exposed structure. It is present in the glass caught in the metalwork, in the ceramic-tile floor, in the simple monochrome paint on the walls, in the standard doors, in the washbasin exhibited in the entrance, in the master bedroom's en suite bathroom, in the crampedness of the bedrooms. Le Corbusier used triviality the same way in both a weekend house and social housing projects. There is also promiscuity between masters and servants in modest open spaces.
There is no more hierarchy: new distinctions must be invented. Le Corbusier pulled off a tour de force. He made well-off middle-class people live in bare spaces although their status tended to make them accumulate. Such bareness became chic. Accumulation, on the contrary, unmasks the nouveau riche; everything else is kitsch.
Le Corbusier admitted that the villa Savoye could be surprising. Is it beautiful? Is it practical? To discuss this is of little interest. Only its creator can sum it up in one word: "It is an object," he declared, implying that it is the logical result of an argument. It is a process. As an object, it is extremely ambitious as to its performance and pragmatic as to its construction.
When visiting the villa, one sometimes runs into visitors exhausting themselves, tape measure in hand, surveying everything: they are certainly trying to uncover secret connections, magical dimensions, winning formulas in the *jeux savants* of architecture. A waste of time! The villa, rough and frank, is a machine of its era. Besides, it leaks. This is a moving weakness, like the oil leaking from the engines of the time, cleared up by stoic and loving drivers.

**Shadow on the ramp.**

**Window onto roof garden and living room.**

58

Living room seen from the terrace.

Ground floor, stairway and ramp.

*Opposite page:* Living room and solarium terrace.

*Opposite page:* Hallway leading to the bedrooms.

*Following pages:* Living room, terrace and access ramp to the solarium.

Living room seen from the terrace.

Living room, view west.

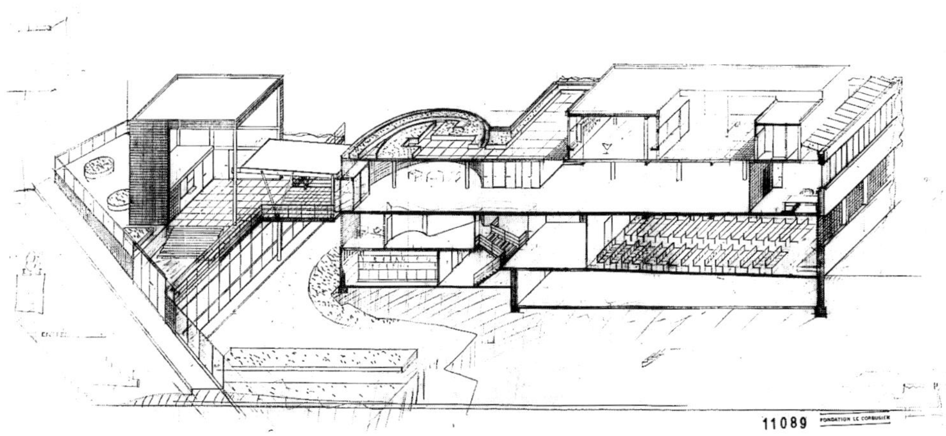

11089

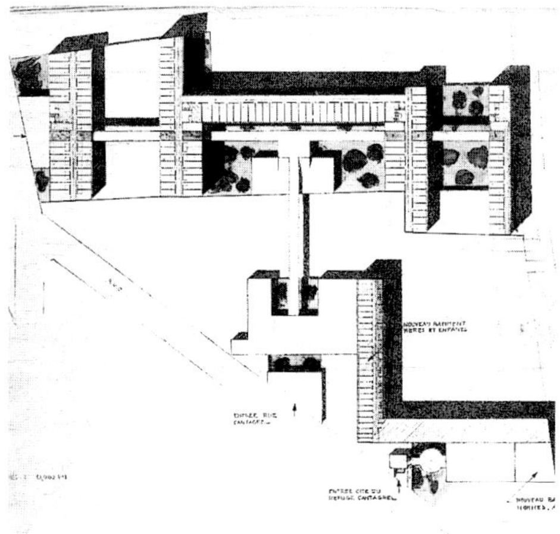

Le Corbusier met Winaretta de Polignac-Singer as part of the circle of friends of his brother Albert Jeanneret, a musician. An active figure in the musical milieu of the 20s, the princesse, of American descent, was a patron of the arts. She was seduced by the project the architect presented to her in July 1926. The villa Polignac was contemporary to the first drafts of villas for the Americans William Cook (Boulogne-Billancourt, 1926-1927) and Michael and Sarah Stein (Vaucresson, 1926-1928), but it was never built. However, the Princess was to act as the ideal go-between for Le Corbusier and the Salvation Army.

She helped Le Corbusier win three contracts of increasing size that followed one after the other: the addition to the Palais du peuple on rue des Cordelières (a three-story house on *pilotis* with a roof terrace) in 1926-1927; the transformation of the boat *Louise-Catherine* into a floating shelter, docked on the Seine at the foot of the viaduct of the Metro station Gare d'Austerlitz in 1929-1930; and finally, in 1929-1933, the Cité de refuge, rue Cantagrel, for an estimated 6 million francs, half of which was donated by the princesse de Polignac; the other half was money collected by the Salvation Army.

Behind a glass and steel curtain of 1,000 square meters, on five floors of dormitories facing south, Le Corbusier imagined a hermetically sealed world, in full light, without any openings or windows: the Cité was to use the "precise breathing" of air conditioning during winter or summer. The architect had to fight to defend these principles. From May 1929 until March 1931, when construction started, five projects followed in succession. Indeed the program changed along the way – the steep plot bought on rue Cantagrel was enlarged by an additional piece of land on rue Chevaleret. Although Paul-Henri Nénot, president of the Conseil général des bâtiments civils, was opposed to the dimensions of the project, the building permit was finally granted in April 1931 in return for a couple of concessions: set-back terraces on the rue Chevaleret and the incline of the glass wall. There was also a bit of cheating: the permit mentions openings that do not exist.

Despite his stubbornness, as well as for budgetary reasons, Le Corbusier did not get air conditioning, but a mechanical ventilation system instead. The central heating worked fine in the winter. But, from the very first summer on, a stuffy kind of heat pervaded in the rooms on the upper floors. The architect continued to resist. Two years later, in 1935, an injunction was delivered by the police authorities to make openings for windows in each bay in under forty days.



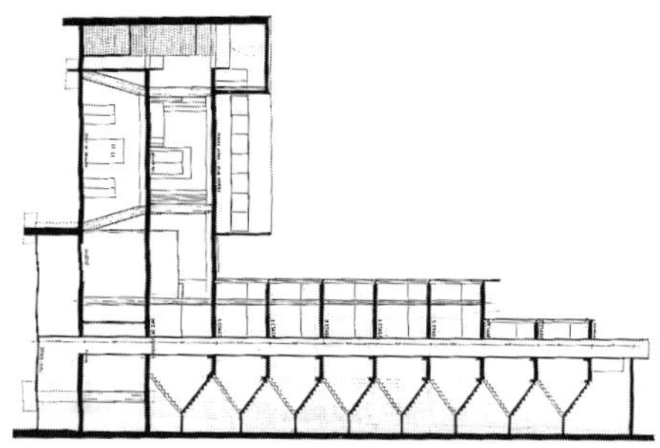

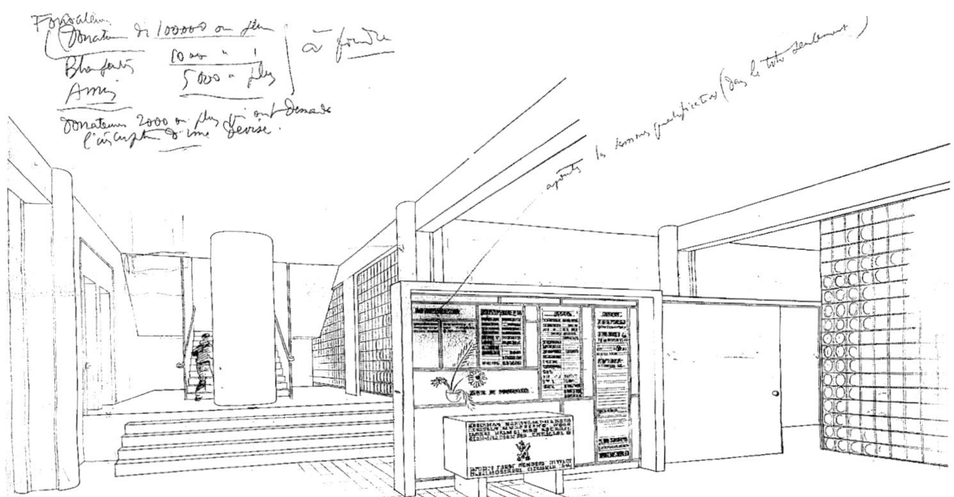

11052

# Cité de refuge

**Project architects:** Le Corbusier and Pierre Jeanneret.
**Client:** Salvation Army, represented by Albin Peyron, general commissioner of the Salvation Army for France and Belgium.
**Construction dates:** 1929-1933.
**Description:** Welfare center including three kinds of services: night shelter (680 beds in dormitories and bedrooms), canteens and workshops. The center also provides daycare services for single mothers and medical care.
**Location:** 12, rue Cantagrel (main entrance) and rue Chevaleret, Paris, 13th arrondissement.
**Current condition:** The building was restored and modified in 1948-1952 under the supervision of Le Corbusier (replacement of the glass curtain damaged by the bombings of August 1944, addition of *brise-soleil*, replacement of the central heating system, redecoration of the lobby). The Cité was entirely repainted in 1975.

In the West, it has long been thought that cities grew in the same way as living organisms: following an indubitable process. According to this principle, maturity provided them with a common framework – articulated around streets, avenues, squares, parks – and a system that lined up the fronts of buildings, pushed them back in places, sometimes diluted them with other elements. An emperor, a king, the pressure of real estate, population influx, chance and casualness could all influence the process or organize it depending on particular interests: these were only simple variations. The system endured, cities had found their layout. There were tortuous organisms, immense bodies, limbs that had grown too quickly, sumptuous forms, botched appendixes, grey complexions, happy disorders, terrible giants, picturesque midgets. All of this was organized around a circulatory system – the street – and kept as close as possible to it, so as not to lose a crumb. Because, on the street, everyone walked by, everything mixed, thus creating a complexity such that, by fermentation, an almost ineluctable second nature appeared: the nature of cities.
But the city overflowed once it became industrialized and its nature entailed catastrophes. It was less loved after that.
It was criticized: a nature which generates too many vices must be civilized. Applying intelligence to it became a matter of urgency. The city was believed to be indisputable in principle: now one wanted to reason with it. It was to be entirely devoted to thought: town planning became a discipline looking for a scientific basis. Much was expected of this new field: managed with gusto, it would produce numerous theories, most of which would be marked by a strong dose of radicalism. Projecting the modern city: this was definitely the goal of urban theories since everyone agreed that the era both irremediably attacked the nature of traditional cities and advanced tremendously.
Le Corbusier, who had a quick wit and a large capacity for enthusiasm, was lavish with general ideas and not the least bit radical when it came to putting cities in sync with their time.
No doubt, he was not the only architect to compose entire cities – making a clean sweep of the past and pretending to cover everything up – but he was the most successful at integrating these huge problems. The least of his achievements sought to provide support for his urban theories and each one represented an opportunity to make the "radiant city" germinate. The continuity of his thought is remarkable.
Thus, the Cité de refuge is as much a work of modern architecture, modest in size, as a test plot for the immeasurable modern city.
By nature, modernity is intransigent. It does not want to compromise with the historical city. By finding its bearings, the Cité de refuge seeks

*Previous pages:* **View from rue Cantagrel.**

to dissolve Paris whose soul is in its streets. In return, Paris and progress would underhandedly dilute some of the Corbusian radicalism.

The street constitutes a frame that is too restraining, too ambiguous, too strongly marked by history, to satisfy modern architecture. Modern architecture is in a hurry to withdraw from this frame, claiming the independence of rational thought and artistic freedom. In the same way, it uses urgency as a pretext to make up social theories quickly from succinct notes on the state of technical progress. The continuity of his thought is remarkable.

The Cité de refuge, in all freedom, does away with the system of streets. It cuts into the street sideways and runs counter to its built-up neighbors, refusing to quietly link their facades. It declines to join the dance. Oblique, it offers the narrowest of facades on the rue Cantagrel – a minimum concession to the obligatory building-line – and deigns to build a narrow strip on the rue Chevaleret.

It is not, however, a question of disappearing. If one disdains the decorum of the street, one is obliged to provide a substitute spectacle. What does one see then?

To have a better view, it is necessary to accompany Le Corbusier by plane. From the air, the city appeared to him like a clutter of forms organized in a way that was obscure to the pilot flying above it. Back on the ground, Le Corbusier wrote: "The plane indicts the city." The implication being that the illusions of the street are revealed by the airplane: the muddled cities are beyond the grasp of modern thinking which thrives on preciseness.

**Southern facade and reception pavilion.**

On the other hand, the pilot can immediately spot the Cité de refuge: a parallelepiped, a cylinder and a cube – a whole that constitutes a landmark with neat lines. From the ground, it is a rational landscape, an arrangement of volumes, their elementary geometry carefully underlined: the parallelepiped is set on a *pilotis* and its lower side is visible; the cube, set on a vast plateau, proudly shows off its twelve even edges; the cylinder descends to a courtyard and stretches out downwards; there is a perfunctory attachment, a footbridge just barely touches it for fear of altering its fresh geometry.

Something radical is at play here: the stakes being to substitute abstraction for representation, working drawings for images and reason for the street.

On more than one level, the street is the place where the show goes on. More than an exhibition place, it is a theater where everyone passes by, meets, makes exchanges. There, one counts upon luck, discovery and chance. One gets thrown out onto the street, cursing fate, violence or promiscuity. The street is the manifestation of the urban condition where the human condition is expressed on all levels. It is such a garrulous theater, so accustomed to trends, revolutions, pretentiousness and decline, that the clear and definitive ideas of the moderns seem but yet another jolt, a recurring inflation of the will to regulate everything, to explain everything. The street puts things in perspective, digests, compromises and enjoys itself. But the moderns want fresh terms: they demand rapt attention from their audience. According to them, nothing can be played on an old set: passions have changed.

In order to set the framework for a modern city, it is necessary to do away with the old scenery including the facades lining the streets. These are planes on which pictures and metaphors are stuck according to trends in decorating, architectural styles, conventions and fashions. Contradictory representations meet without too much concern. Sometimes there is nothing and the scenery evokes poverty. Sometimes ostentation reigns along entire boulevards and the exuberance of the decor suggests a wealthiness proud of showing off, far from the tyranny of good taste. These devices are expressed less by the volume than by the facing, less by the space than by the atmosphere. The atmosphere of the street. An ambiguous term: atmosphere is elusive.

Volume, however, is clearly defined by geometry. It suits the modern architect's purpose to organize,with the rigor of strict mathematical rules, the world into a logical system where illusions are obsolete.

Not only a talented geometrician, Le Corbusier also sought to touch the soul, seat of the emotions. He left space around the volumes of the Cité de refuge. The individual walks along the Cité as along a metaphysical stroll. The relationships between the platonic forms found there bear witness to the immanent presence of a rational mind guided by geometry and the ambition to measure everything. The spirit is in the empty spaces. The space between the volumes becomes as important as the volumes themselves.

Volume and space are modern inventions that ignore the street, its events, its scenery. Man may be disenchanted, but he is completely new.

The Cité de refuge is an alternative to the linearity of traditional urban spaces. By keeping a distance, its volumes indicate that they are their own masters and produce their own effects. They make the air circulate around them in order to open up to the pedestrian. Their abstract character shapes the sensibility of the stroller to make him a protagonist of modernity despite himself.

Here, abstraction, which replaces the world of pictures, takes on a decidedly graphic and colorful turn.

The facades of the Cité de refuge are regulated by patterns, lines and

**Reception.**

View of the access by the covered footbridge.

grids on which typography and areas of pure color find a place. This aesthetic system produces a spectacular landscape capable of assuming the scale of a urban complex. Perfectly mastered, the spectacle evokes the strong presence of a creator, of an organizer.
Le Corbusier, freed from urban conventions, also turned his back on his previous works : white, prismatic, "purist" villas. In the Cité de refuge, the graphic work designs ambiguous volumes, lightens up what is grounding, breaks the continuity of solid bodies, frees their planes, favors the page, what is written, by installing discontinuity. The sides of the building are made of clear or frosted glass, glass bricks and sometimes, nothing. This treatment blurs the usual limits between interior and exterior, between things and the space between them, between the incoming light and the surrounding light. Where one expected an univocal architecture, clearly defined by the play of the volumes, one is confronted with a complex work – full of unforeseen circumstances – that is difficult to grasp. Emotion finds satisfaction in these breaks, although they constitute a terrible test for those who continued Le Corbusier's work.
These aesthetic considerations were only some of Le Corbusier's preoccupations. He focused his energies on the organization of the modern city: his chief concern was the fate of people in the city. He was perfectly skilled at directing the features of urban life to people his projects, to inhabit his theories.
The Cité de refuge was commissioned by the Salvation Army. Its role is to give shelter to those that life has damaged and thrown onto the streets. Le Corbusier took this aim further: getting the homeless off the streets was not enough, he would literally remove them from the street by placing them in an environment that was autonomous and controlled to the point of becoming perfectly airtight.
The rooms, placed in the parallelepiped, have no contact with the exterior, their glazed facades are hermetically sealed. To ensure comfort, Le Corbusier invented a vocabulary for want of a technology: the "breathing wall" and "precise breathing" control the amount of sunlight and ventilation. It did not work. However, the technology did exist: air conditioning was starting to be developed in the United States. But Le Corbusier dealt with the purely technical problem of controlling the atmosphere in an offhand way. As an artist, he only trusted his intuitions, even if they were technical; as an ideologist, he did not worry about the warnings of the engineers when they questioned his hypotheses. However, his theories – some of which are social in nature – always rely on "scientific" arguments in order to attain their universal dimension. By resorting to abstraction, the Cité de refuge sought to establish the

**Stairway leading to upper floors.**

**Reception with glass block partition wall.**

features of a standard building, unchanging, easily transposable to all latitudes, whatever the characteristics of the climates involved and the hazards of meteorology. The building was also a laboratory where social experiments were conducted in ideal conditions. The modern building would ideally be inhabited by a sample of people who had burst all their bonds. Tramps and lost souls were supposed to rebuild a life for themselves on this oasis of organized life that was a perfect "social condenser." They would be reborn by moving in the Cité de refuge's purified atmosphere which spared them the miasma of the streets and protected them from the unpredictability of the historic city. The Cité de refuge sheltered an experiment in seclusion.

To a certain extent, abstraction, social welfare and the exercise of will are worrying.

Technology was to have its revenge. It was roasting hot inside the Cité de refuge and Le Corbusier had no choice but to fit the facade with *brise-soleil* that altered the delicacy of the original composition. Paris played a part in this by imposing setbacks on the upper levels and openings in the facades. Le Corbusier resented all of this bitterly. What did it matter? For him these mishaps were but a temporary fog, an unavoidable rain-shower. The bright sun of glorious days to come was to shine even stronger.



**Detail of coating and glass blocks.**

***Opposite page:* Facade on rue Chevaleret.**

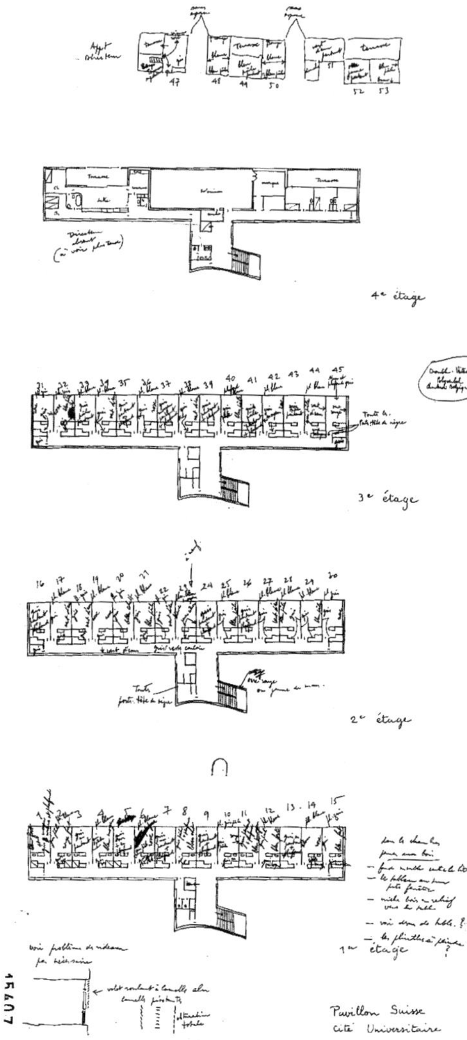


Offering students decent and cheap accommodation, developing their taste for hygiene and socializing, teaching young people from different countries, from different cultures and walks of life to live together: these were the goals of Emile Deutsch de la Meurthe, founder of the Cité universitaire internationale. Le Corbusier echoed these sentiments. In 1925, in the margins of a theoretical study for a student residence: "All students have the right to the same unit, it should be cruel for the unit of the poor to be different from that of the rich [. . .] each unit has its own entranceway, kitchen, toilet, main room, garret for sleeping and roof garden."

Four years later, in the Cité universitaire de Paris, the architect materialized these thoughts on student housing: the pavillon suisse offers about fifty bedrooms, 6 meters deep with a 2.8 meter facade, with sink, shower and closet space. Each "cellule-tiroir" (drawer-cell) is soundproofed and independent of the structure, a three-story "maison-boîte" (box-house) set on pillars. The minimal units of the pavillon suisse prefigure those of the preaching friars at the monastery of la Tourette (1953-1961), and their arrangement, like a " bottle rack," that of the Cité radieuse in Marseilles (1945-1952), which has been evoked so often.

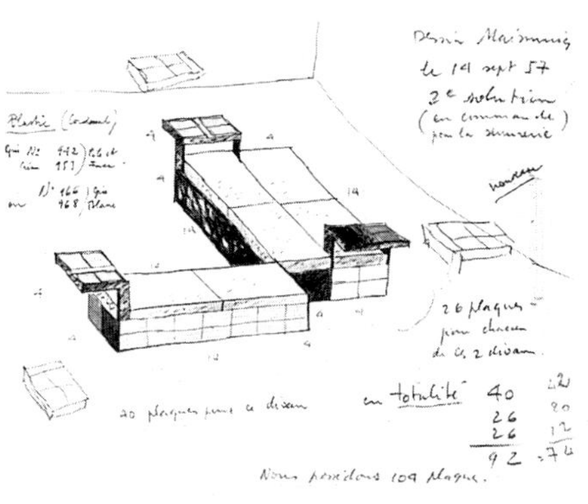

After the repudiation of the League of Nations competition in Geneva (1927), when Le Corbusier had just been granted French citizenship (1930), the Swiss contract was (almost) easy: President Rudolph Fueter was enthusiastic (Le Corbusier would design a villa for him in 1950), and the contract was supported by some of the architects biggest champions: Raoul La Roche, Karl Moser and Siegfried Giedion. However, because of the insistency of the curatorium's members and of Doctor Ritter from the Technische Hochschule in Zurich, the project underwent certain changes, namely in terms of the load-bearing structure: the four skimpy steel posts of the first project became six sturdy solid concrete *pilotis*. Seven rooms for French students were also added to the forty planned initially; they occupy part of the roof, which lost its solarium in the process.

Twenty years later, in the center of the same Cité universitaire, Le Corbusier constructed the pavillon du Brésil (1953-1959), based on the preliminary drawing of Brazilian architect Lucio Costa.

# Pavillon suisse

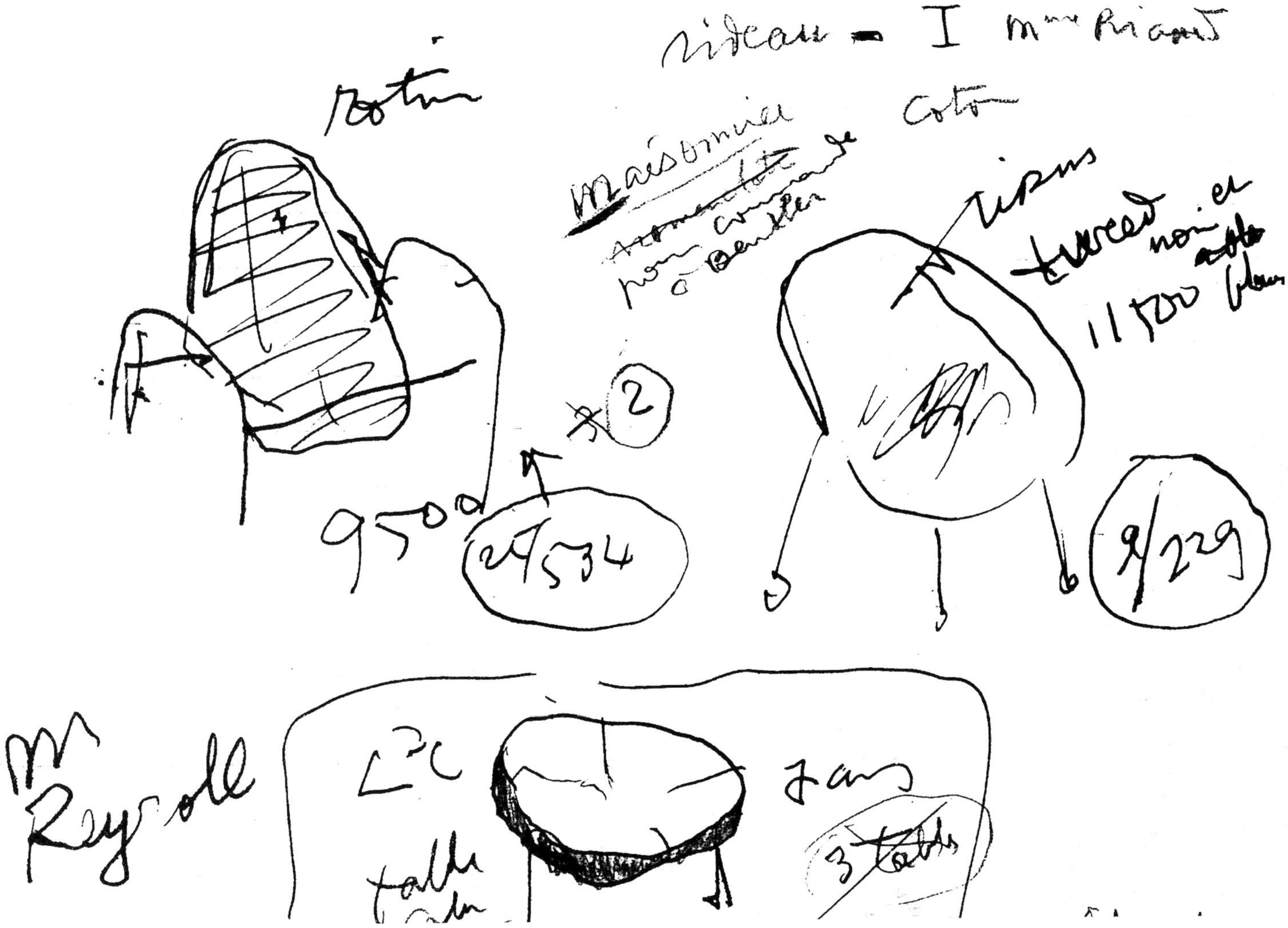




**Project architects:** Le Corbusier and Pierre Jeanneret.

**Client:** Swiss Universities Committee represented by the curatorium of the Maison suisse of the Cité universitaire in Paris under the presidency of Professor Rudolph Fueter.

**Construction dates:** 1929-1933.

**Description:** Student residence with refectory for breakfast, bathrooms on every floor, meeting rooms, directors' apartments and caretaker's lodge.

**Location:** Cité universitaire internationale, Paris, 14th arrondissement. The entrance is on 7, boulevard Jourdan.

**Current condition:** The pavillon was enriched by a mural done by Le Corbusier in 1948. In the 50s, the facade was restored (insulation work was done and venetian blinds were hung), the living room was redecorated (enamels after drawings by Le Corbusier), and the bedrooms were painted vivid colors.

Southern facade overlooking the park.

*Opposite page:* Entrance and access stairway to the floor above.

Student lounge.

# Time works differently from one country

to another – from Denmark to Cambodia, from Morocco to Argentina, from Mexico to the Netherlands – but...

Although they are singled out by their regional or historical styles, the national pavilions of the Cité internationale de Paris share essential characteristics that history and geography agree upon: their quietness is reassuring, their stability has been proven. They owe these qualities to the use of traditional materials, the thickness of their walls, the evenness of their openings and to a picturesque quality that gently informs the stroller about their differences without appearing too bizarre.

Their facades are clothes that hide the approximations and immodesty of private life. They give a dignified quality to daily order, take on passions and temper crises. They allow enough shadow for current disorders to quickly return to the realm of memory. The proof being that none of the famous Hyperborean angst troubles the serenity of the facades of the pavillon suisse's Swedish and Danish neighbors.

Switzerland, a peaceful country, remained neutral during international conflicts. Here, it logically chose to avoid any confrontation between nations and to dress internationally. That is to say, modernly. Switzerland thus put itself in a paradoxical situation. As representing modernity is not a tranquil position, the pavillon suisse is distinguished by its lack of tranquility. The pavillon is strained. In front of its neighbors, well-placed houses, it detaches its body from the ground, lifting it to place it on a narrow concrete base. There, it maintains an impressive balance. This spectacle produces an emotion comparable to the astonishment felt when watching a gymnast performing an exercise. The preciseness and the precarious mastery involved are disquieting. A bit more to the right, a bit more to the left, and the pure parallelepiped, which constitutes the main part of the pavillon, would fall headfirst. Swiss precision ensures the equilibrium, but the effects produced by the modern sensibility are unsettling nonetheless.

The pavillon shamelessly shows itself off. While its neighbors, covering up their respective residents, hide the blurred outlines of their lives to better communicate the notions of permanency and wholeness, the pavillon chooses to be extroverted, split up and fragmented. It exposes its parts. It uses everything as an excuse for disjunction: each of its functional units, singled out by a distinctive material, tackles its neighbor. Le Corbusier did not practise the arts of blending or allusion which make for the pleasantness of middle-class conversations. He made statements: the world is a complex machine, let's inspect its engine. It was done straightforwardly and was easy to grasp: he put the bedrooms on one side of the parallelepiped where he affixed a glass facade. The corridors are on the other side and the facade is marked by the symmetrical openings

of square windows set flush. The stairway constitutes a separate volume. One of its sides features a vertical arrangement of glass blocks, another traces a curve. The living room, placed horizontally on the grass behind a curved millstone wall, opens wide onto a slightly bulging glass pane. The concrete *pilotis* are six powerful elements; the fragile glass prism of the hall delicately slides in between them.

There is no cacophony in this complex combination. Everything was calculated to compose a play of forms to be directed by Le Corbusier. The show is only open to the person whose movements animate the changing relationship between the masses. The pavillon suisse is not suitable material for a postcard; it must be filmed. The show is performed by real actors. The empty spaces are staged as much as the solids. In the empty spaces outlined by the volumes – that is, in the private space – the residents stand before the audience. Their privacy is nonexistent because their life is visible from all sides: it is projected through the glass facades of the bedrooms, living room or hall and diffused by the glass blocks. Nothing is left unsaid, nothing is hidden, it is not clear however if the people living there are supposed to behave and put up a front, their aloofness replacing the traditional mask of constructed objects, or if – provided they are given the opportunity, in the absence of shadows – they are to break free of conventional behaviour and overact their liberated intimacy. (Schindler used to dance on the roof of his Los Angeles – a modern city – villa in the nude. But Schindler was Viennese.)

The pavillon suisse is a liberated work. It ends the period of "white villas" which constitute a cerebral series, yearning for the absolute and subjected to precise rules. Taking a radical stance for one's whole life is in itself a remarkable attitude. But keeping to fixed rules runs the risk of generating boredom and dogmatism. To avoid growing prematurely old, it is a good idea to make fun of one's own precepts and to explore new fields. A register is imposed on the inventor: that of irony, play and distance. Le Corbusier had a fine mind. As a hurried architect, he naturally understood that once the rules have been laid down, their range would quickly be exhausted. So he had fun placing curves where no one expected him to, less to play with the light – Le Corbusier is too easily credited with sublime intentions – than to transgress his own rules and mark out a new territory. He toyed with a millstone wall, with the organic forms of the *pilotis*, used the tremendously liberating effects of fracture, assembled materials with much vigor and created shocking transparencies. Beyond the limits he had set for himself, he pushed briefly toward deconstruction, but lastingly toward sensuality.

Le Corbusier enjoyed himself with the pavillon suisse. Which of his present-day followers can say he is having fun?

**Entrance pavilion.**

***Opposite page:*** **Entrance lobby.**

***Following pages:*** **Facade overlooking the park.**

**Entrance pavilion, western facade.**

In his foreword to the third edition of *Vers une architecture,* dated January 1, 1928, Le Corbusier, who was excluded from the contest for the League of Nations building in Geneva, voiced his anger about the academism and conservatism of respectable society and of the candidates in the competition for the "representative mausoleum." He wrote, "Modern society is being completely remodelled while the League of Nations retreats behind the curtain." Geneva did not seem to welcome its child prodigy. Nevertheless, a private contract was offered to Le Corbusier two years after his formal repudiation by the League of Nations: located in the city's south-east, Clarté was an experimental apartment building, a descendant of the Corbusian "immeubles-villas," built for Edmond Wanner, an industrialist specializing in building metalworks.

The family business dealing in wrought iron, Wanner & Cie. was founded in 1853 and, at the end of the 20s, was undergoing transformations: not content with its mastery of traditional ironwork, it was also eager to master and patent new methods. In 1927, Edmond Wanner visited the Weissenhof exhibition. This visit quickly led to a correspondence with Le Corbusier, then to highly technical projects. Wanner was both the client and contractor of Clarté, for which he designed and built the cast-steel frame; Wanner & Cie also provided the elements of the site's glass and steel facade, including the sliding windows, named "Wanner windows."

After this undertaking in Geneva, which did however lose a planned extension that was never completed for budgetary reasons, Le Corbusier continued to call on the industrialist, whether for precise contracts (manufacturing sliding windows for the pavillon suisse at the Cité universitaire de Paris in 1932; manufacturing revolving doors for the building at 24, rue Nungesser-et-Coli in 1933), or for more doubtful financial and real estate deals (project for porte Molitor, Paris, in 1931; Invalides building, Paris, 1932-1935).

Coming after the villas built during Le Corbusier's formative years in Le Locle and La Chaux-de-Fonds, after the little house in Corseaux on Lake Geneva, the Clarté building was the architect's last project in Switzerland. Projects designed at the beginning of the 30s did not see the light of day: in Geneva, the Mundaneum world museum (1929) and the urbanization plans for the right bank (1933); in Zurich, the apartment house at Zurichhorn (1932) and the building on Rentenanstalt (1933). However, in 1967, Heidi Weber constructed, after Le Corbusier's death, a "maison de l'Homme" – based on a 1964 project – in Zurich. The building, called Centre Le Corbusier-Heidi Weber, draws on Le Corbusier's dreams for a "pavilion for a synthesis of the arts." It also gives a hint as to what the "museum for the visual arts" – which, in 1949-1951 almost came into existence on the grounds once occupied by Luna Park, porte Maillot, Paris – might have been.

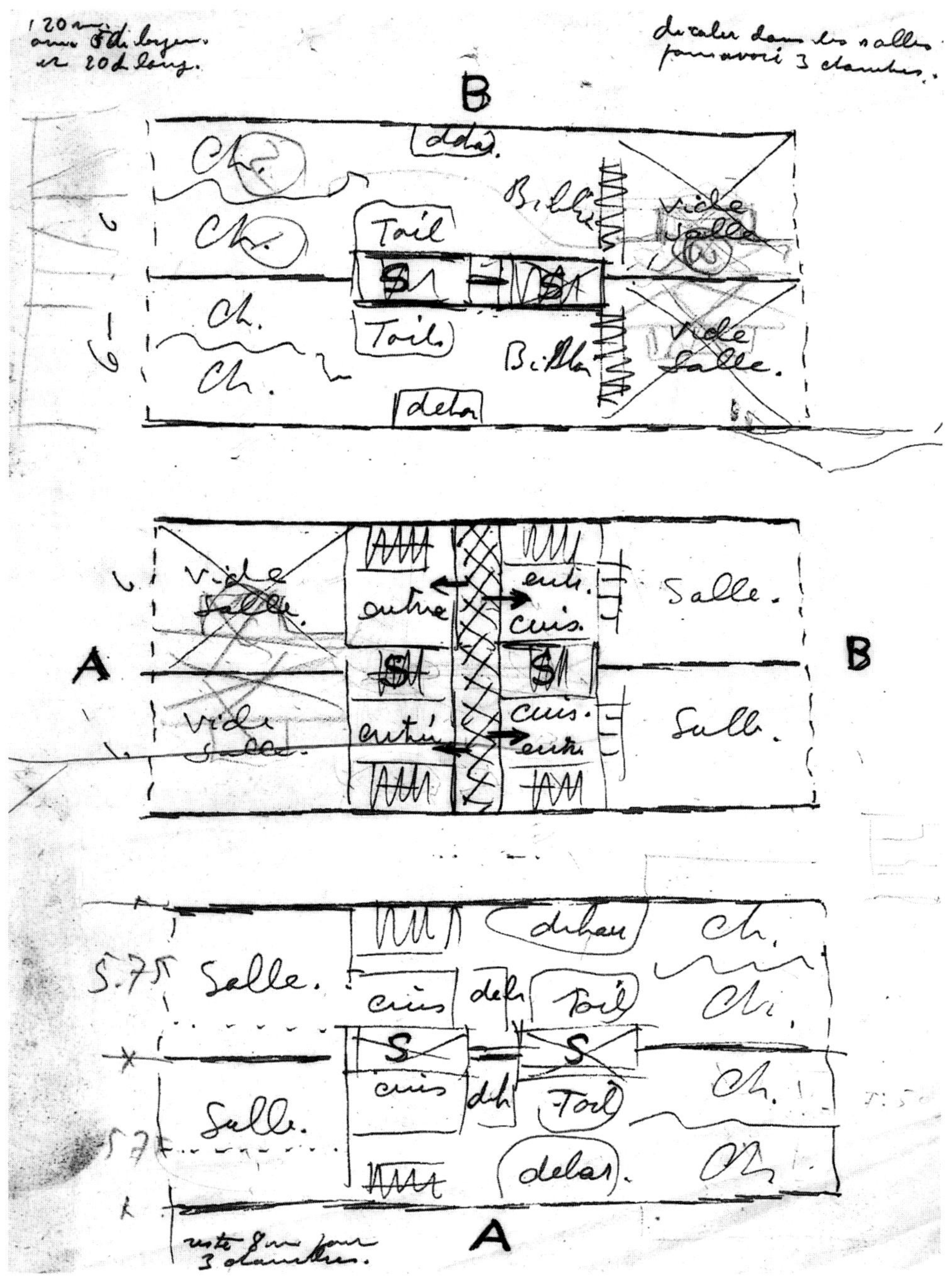

# Clarté building

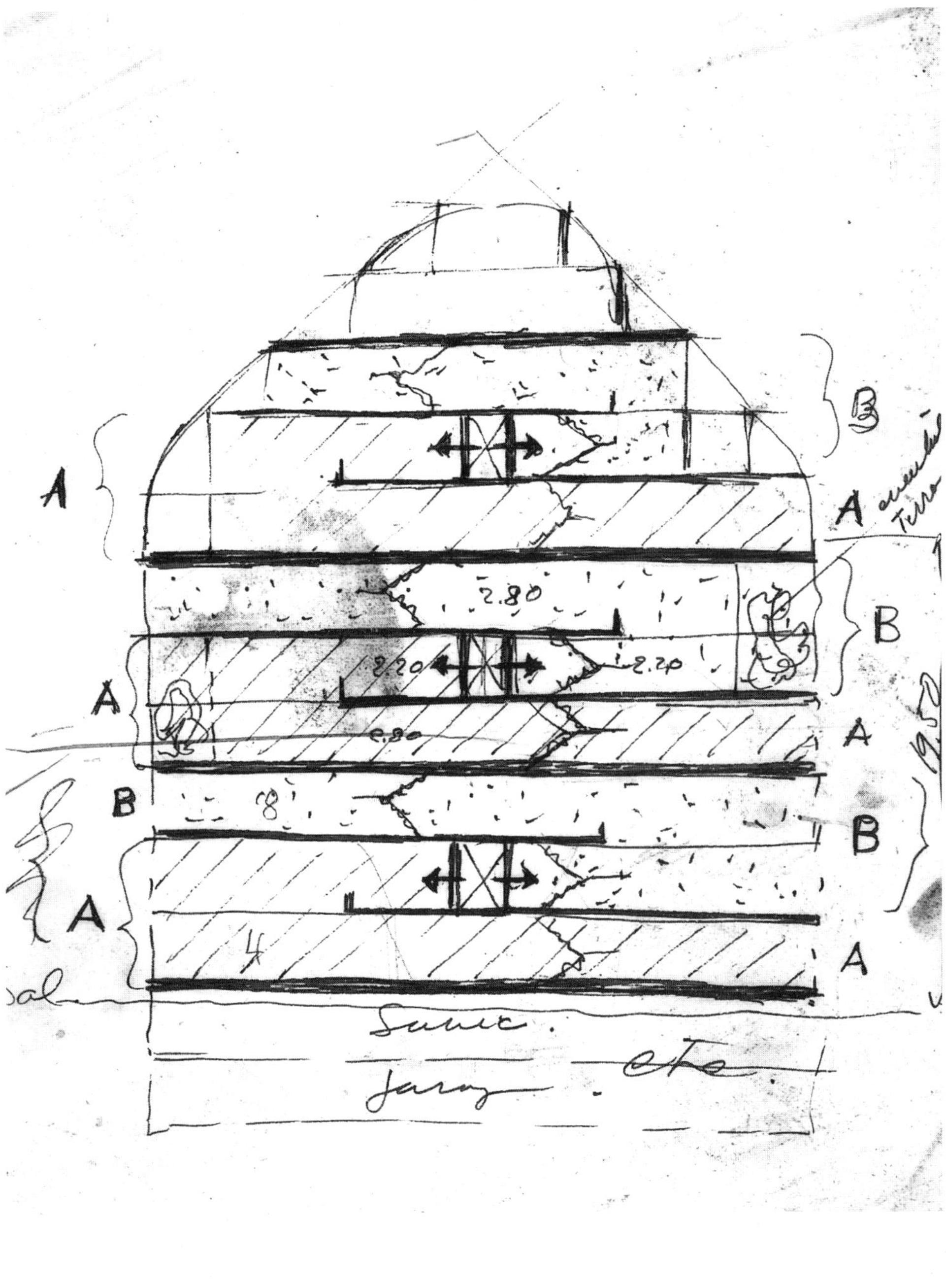


**Project architects:** Le Corbusier and Pierre Jeanneret, with the active participation of the client.
**Client:** Edmond Wanner (1898-1965), Genevan industrialist.
**Construction dates:** 1930-1932.
**Description:** Apartment building of 45 duplex units.
**Location:** 2, rue Saint-Laurent, 1207 Geneva, Switzerland.

The building in the city.

Opposite page: Southwestern facade, balconies and blinds.

At a given time in a given place, human settlement reaches such a level that a city is born. Urban settlements may be divided into two main categories. Horizontal cities welcome people living quietly next to each other in individual houses with little gardens. Vertical cities, full of excitement, are overflowing with residents living on top of each other in high-rise apartment buildings.

Very early on, Le Corbusier tuned his architecture to the vast areas of reflection that reformulated the rules of urban settlement and community life. Although he was fond of greenery, he denounced the horizontal city as a waste of space that was contrary to the spirit of modern urban civilization. He also wanted to reform the vertical city which was congested, anonymous, too directly determined by real estate profits and did not provide the "essential pleasures": sun, space and nature.

The Clarté apartment building offered a solution for this contradictory ambition: since it was not possible to build cities in the countryside, on natural ground, artificial grounds would be created in the city in order to set up an ersatz countryside there.

The Clarté building piles up a series of duplex apartments and lengthens them by balconies deep enough to contain all the comfort, greenery and imagination generally found in suburban backyards. The dimensions of the building are doubled by the balconies and the scale of the neighboring buildings is diminished. The city gets a second wind there. Its affability is also increased. Perched on these large balconies, hidden behind the fabric of the large orange blinds, the signs of daily life take a more generous and noble turn than usual. The apartment building has the dimensions of a palace: one feels tall there. It has the dimensions of a cruise ship: one is swept along by a powerful movement. With very little effort, daily luxury is made accessible and the enjoyment of ordinary things becomes a show.

However, the building stands alone in the heart of a city which makes its living by producing luxuries. Geneva undoubtedly prefers not to show off what surpasses strict economy and the Clarté building remains a curiosity even though it would like to serve as a model.

What about elsewhere? It did not serve as an example of reasonably luxurious apartment buildings either. Why? The reservations had nothing to do with cost or profitability, so they could only have been cultural in nature. In 1930, the Clarté apartment building established new standards of comfort and provided architects with a fresh, attractive and generous alternative. However, they did not let themselves be convinced. In their eyes, immeuble Clarté was not architecture.

They were right. The logic in the conception of the Clarté building is

that of design. It does not allow itself to be influenced by any cultural prejudices and the building owes nothing to history or to the geography of styles. It does not mistake identity for culture, Geneva style with the duty of intelligence.

The building is filled with an interior logic that belongs more to the design of objects than to architectural practice. It is a mechanism, an artefact intended to be mass-produced rather than a work created to comfort the "natural" identity of a place.

The Clarté building is based on an analysis of human needs and the technical abilities of the construction industry; it demonstrates a concern with improving them. The building sets itself goals: modularity, planes freed of load-bearing walls by a post/beam/light facade structure, apartments with double orientation, double-height, large manageable bay windows, deep balconies, a planted terrace, an integrated garage and so on.

The building's appearance is that of a perfectly executed process. The smallest details are designed to be useful. From the facade panels to the clasps of the blinds, everything seeks lightness. All of the details demonstrate the same attention and indicate the same concern for preciseness. As the building is well used and well inhabited, the whole acquires sensuality.

Its aesthetic is not flatly derived from function, but from overcoming it. There is something of the automobile in the Clarté building. The apartment building opens the invigorating paths of design to the architect and offers its inhabitants an enlarged "space."

The Clarté building is a liberating object.

**Southwestern facade.**



***Opposite page:*** **Stairways and landings.**

*Le Corbusier in his studio, rue Nungesser-et-Coli (1960).*

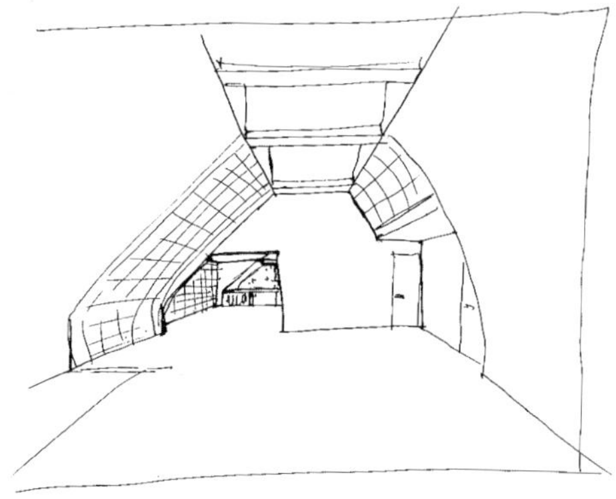

"Apartments for subscription... Unique location... Tennis, swimming pool, racetrack, hockey." At the beginning of 1932, the real estate firm SIPP raved about the nearby sports facilities and outdoors activities (bois de Boulogne, Jean-Bouin and Roland-Garros stadiums, the velodrome at parc des Princes, the Molitor swimming pool) in its advertising brochure and also unveiled Le Corbusier and Jeanneret's glass facade outlined in black. In February 1932, construction began on a plot between rue Nungesser-et-Coli and rue de la Tourelle. Le Corbusier had thought he could build on the whole lot (he started by submitting the project of an "immeuble-villa" to the Genevan industrialist Edmond Wanner). Two buildings constructed in 1931, one in white stone and the other of stone and brick in the Art Deco style, coped the Corbusian building and compelled it to share common courtyards.

The SIPP commission is dated June 1931. The constraint was that the plot was only 13 meters wide and 26 meters deep. The apartments could not have a double orientation, they would have to be back to back, each opening on one facade. The east-west orientation and the location – with unimpeded views – at one of loveliest gateways to Paris were exceptional.

From the start, the architects decided on twin facades, with glass fronts that let light in. Before then, glass was used solely for public buildings (offices, exhibition pavilions, etc.) and had been seldom used for housing. Thus, along with the glass house of Doctor Dalsace built by Pierre Chareau in 1931, the building at number 24 was a pioneer.

Another original aspect of the assignment was the "freedom" granted to the buyers: size of the apartment, number of rooms, layout of the interior, all were offered "tailored according to the purchaser's wishes." This flexibility, which materialized with Le Corbusier's "open plan," broke completely with the traditional layout of middle-class apartments. Functionality, transparency and ingeniousness feature. The duplex at number 24 is topped by a double vaulted roof (house and studio) and furnished with the help of Charlotte Perriand (partition-wall/furniture in the kitchen, dressing-table/screen in the bedroom, etc.) made the Le Corbusiers the first "radiant citizens" of Paris.

For this project, the architect launched into the torments of real estate. He agreed – under the terms of the contract with the SIPP developers who lacked funds from the start – to look for buyers himself. Fernand Léger, André Maurois, Jean Wiener, Arthur Honegger, Doctor Winter, François de Pierrefeu, among others, were approached. In 1934, Le Corbusier even tried his luck with the writer James Joyce. The following year, SIPP went bankrupt, starting a legal and financial imbroglio that would only be resolved after the war, in 1949. Le Corbusier lived in his apartment illegally for over fifteen years. In return for the sale of a Picasso and a Braque, his rights as joint tenant were finally established.



B 2979 COUPE B-B.

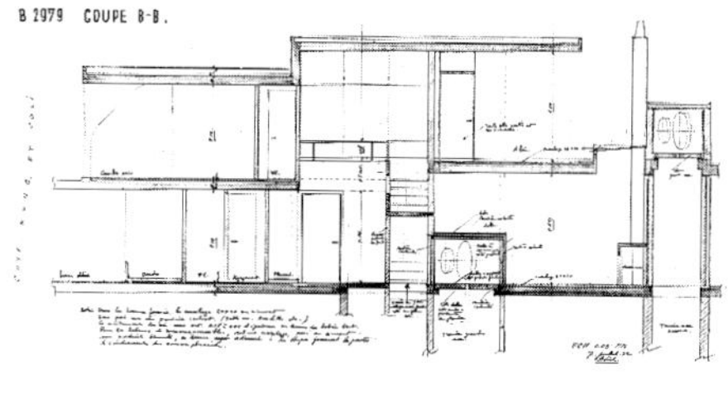

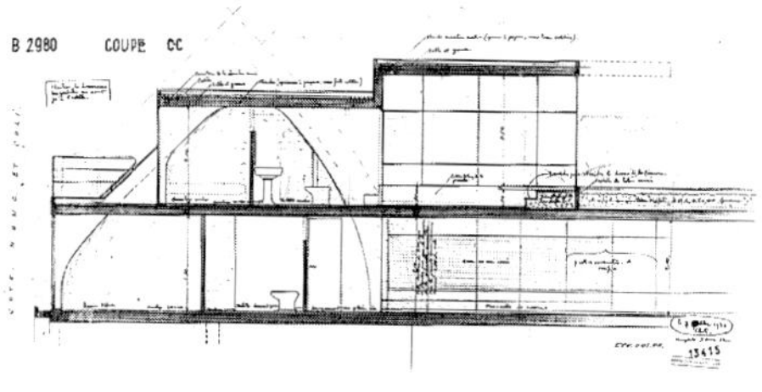

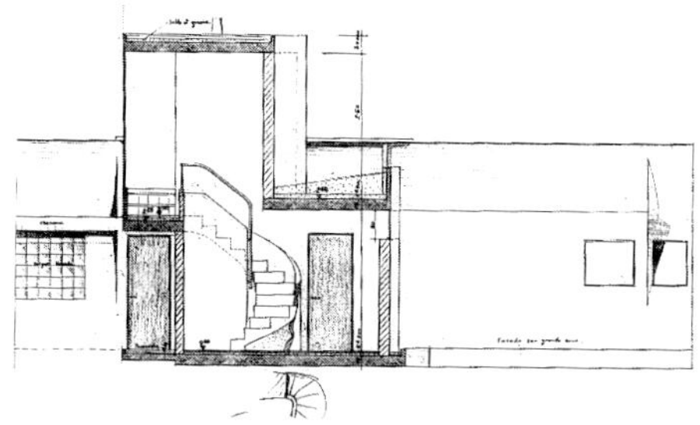

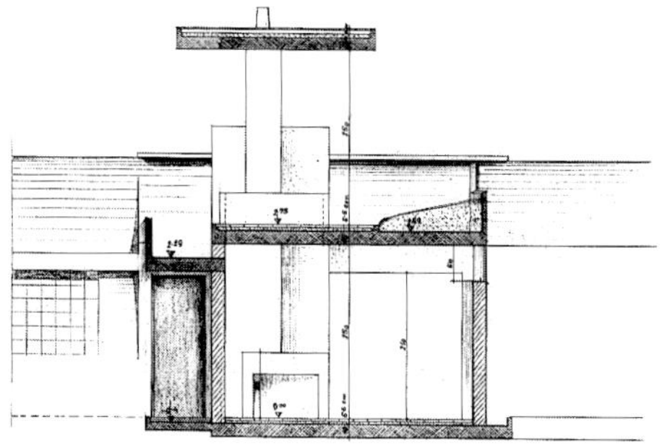

# Nungesser-et-Coli building

**Project architects:** Le Corbusier and Pierre Jeanneret. Charlotte Perriand collaborated on the fitting-out of Le Corbusier's apartment.
**Client:** Société immobilière de Paris-Parc des Princes (SIPP), represented by Mr. Kousnetzoff and Mr. Noble, and Mr. and Mrs. Le Corbusier.
**Construction dates:** 1931-1934.
**Description:** Apartment house on seven and eight levels (eight on the east facade, rue Nungesser-et-Coli; seven on the west facade, rue de la Tourelle), with balconies and central bay window, with two or three apartments on each floor, 110-120 square meters in size, on the first six levels. Floors 7 and 8 are set back and were Le Corbusier's "house on top of the house" – his duplex apartment and studio, with roof terrace.
**Location:** 24, rue Nungesser-et-Coli, Paris, 16th arrondissement, and rue de la Tourelle, Boulogne-Billancourt, Hauts-de-Seine.
**Current condition:** The frame of the glass wall on the Nungesser-et-Coli side was changed in 1948 (replacement of the metal sections by wooden frames by carpenter and friend Charles Barberis), then again in 1962 (anodized aluminium frames). The apartment/studio belongs to the Fondation Le Corbusier.

*Opposite page:* Entrance facade, rue Nungesser-et-Coli.

It is a developer's building located in a wealthy neighborhood: all black and steel, squeezed in between golden stone buildings built during the same period. They bear a family likeness, a family formally lined up to have their picture taken for a special occasion. They are dressed quite modernly for the occasion. The artist uncle, the intellectual, the eccentric can be spotted at number 24. He has a hand in the pocket of his sports jacket and smiles directly at the camera.

The family accepted his revolutionary opinions as long as he was urbane. Is the building representative of the avant-garde of the "contemporary city" (open plan, open facade, roof terrace, strip window, industrial materials, located close to a park and sporting facilities)? Fine! As long as the revolutionary wind did not mess up his hair, the bourgeois resident of rue Nungesser-et-Coli serenely accepted the omen and left the decision as to the outcome to time. In so doing, he cultivated a hardy soul: no question of altering neighborliness between well-to-do people because of different sensibilities.

On that subject our era is faint-hearted: Paris, for example, is coughing up the supposedly sulphurous smell coming from the mix of stone buildings and glass buildings. This proves that history is cyclical. Le Corbusier thought that, with rue Nungesser-et-Coli, he was advancing a pawn that would play into the modern city's game and, according to domino theory, cover the old city. In fact, he was starting a movement that is now going around in circles.

Well, this was not taken up by the neighborhood. The fuss did not change the ways of the family. The buildings on rue Nungesser-et-Coli did not change their habits and took a disconcerting stand on the modern building, a stand involving true politeness, sincere and learned interest, as well as amusement, distance and even condescension.

No doubt, their position was understandable. Modernity does not take a very pleasing turn for the uninitiated, since it claims responsibility for the break-up. It can be said of this building that it is awesome because it is black and made of glass and iron. What next? It is not easy for the man on the street to spot where the efforts of the architect went or where his talent, draftsmanship, and taste for decoration are expressed.

When it is considered from the point of view of the neighboring buildings, elegant number 24, full of modern freshness, can pass off as falsely naive and clumsy. Its windows are not even expressed and its scale demonstrates a militant simplicity that may be mistaken for too much self-assurance or even pride. To be honest, the spectacle is bold. The facade is fashioned of iron and glass (with a bit of concrete

Rue Nungesser-et-Coli seen from Jean-Bouin Stadium.

Roof terrace looking south.

Dining corner and south balcony.

painted black to simulate metal), black and white as colors, the plane and the parallelepiped as elements of composition, a superimposition of horizontal strips as a rule and that is all. It also happens to be all that is needed to be radically modern. When it is compared to bourgeois representations, it is boring. Was this the work of a visionary man or of a likeable eccentric? The family wondered, but preferred not to take a stand and went back to its comfort. However, the modernity of 24 rue Nungesser-et-Coli compromised with its context. It had to comply with the town-planning rules it rejected because they do not allow the autonomy to which strict modernity aspired. Inside, constrained by two small courtyards, the apartments struggle to fully enjoy the benefits of the open plan. However, free of load-bearing walls, they can be arranged according to their owners' wishes. The most famous owner was Le Corbusier who lived with his wife in an apartment and had a studio on the seventh and eighth floors.

Up there, the modernity that Le Corbusier applied to himself took a particular turn. Certainly, the plan is open, the space is fluid, there is a strip window, the terrace is planted, there is light everywhere, there is a ceramic tile floor, the doors pivot and the walls are multicolored (but just a touch: no doubt, Le Corbusier did not need to spread his artistic feeling all over when he could concentrate his pictorial research in his studio). Indubitably, the treatment is modern. But the tension put into his previous works is not prescribed in his apartment and one should not expect to find emotions regarding the "quality of space" or the "work with light" here. It is not a retreat: it is subtle because it is an accommodating variation on modernity.

One is struck by the realization that, here, the modern touch is applied to fixing leftovers, to arranging the trivial and the contingent to make them, bit by bit, into a work verging on pottering, on something precarious, on do-it-yourself. The modern project, the purist vocabulary, which were thought to have been carefully weighed, thought out and calculated in the smallest details according to an uncompromising artistic sensibility, seem in this case to have gone on vacation.

At home, Le Corbusier did not try to make people believe that he had the recipes needed to transform the world by assigning a precise place to everything. On the contrary, he let things be, took them as they were and had fun with them to the point of making their mere presence seem uncanny.

These things, which the architect accepted without trying to distort them when they imposed themselves on him, were first of all inferred from town-planning rules: height limited to 2.5 meters on the seventh-floor facade, resulting in two vaults in the assigned template. The

**Living room corner and zenith opening.**

Studio.

mandatory set-backs also define the layout of the eighth floor, just as the two courtyards constrain the entrance to the apartment and divide its layout, the shafts of the elevators go through the living room, the slanting post which crosses the large bay-window in the studio. What the architect made the best of among the trivial things include the summarily drafted gable wall, half-stone, half-brick, left bare in the studio; the pipes of all kinds made visible; the lavish amount of sanitary and cooking equipment displayed ostentatiously; and the furniture in the bedroom that evokes the furniture found in dormitories all free of any affect, of any sign of intimacy and reduced to a working drawing.

Two attitudes are mixed here. On the one hand, there is a pronounced taste for a detached way of life, free of middle-class restraints and conventions, that shuns individualism and is tempted by the idea of a rustic community. On the other hand, there is a kind of pleasure that calls for an almost Eastern conception of spirituality, and finds fulfillment in not directing the course of things, in not modifying their arrangements in order to get caught up in the spectacle of their very presence. The sink, the radiators and all their pipes, placed in front of windows or in the middle of glass-block walls, seem to be floating in the air. Against the light, their obviousness is such that they may claim to disappear. To camouflage them would be a heavy gesture and it would be ineffective in the end. It is best to let these elements get to work, not confront them in any way, act as if there is nothing shocking about them and thus profit from the energy of the modern world, let go of the old world's falseness and become inclined to feel new emotions.

With the same detachment, Le Corbusier, philosophically let the forces of nature make up, as the wind blew, a garden on the eighth floor terrace. In the same way, he let his intimate forces and the artistic aspect of his personality express themselves by allowing them to turn his studio into a shambles. Nevertheless, Le Corbusier misled us: he did not leave anything to chance. Rather than a contemplative wise man, he was an active hero who retrieved a part of what seemed to slip away from him by returning it to the order of discourse. In the studio, the gable wall left bare becomes a sermon and brings the modern man, estranged from nature, back in contact with the fatal reality of things, with sensuality and with the healthy vigor of bricklayers. He bestowed upon the vaults outlined by the maximum construction height regulations the obviousness of an architectural paradigm. The elevator shaft, with its carved niches, becomes an abstract sculpture. The sink and the bidet, placed next to modern paintings, establish an edifying connection between art and industry.

The spider has gone back to the center of the web.

Living room
and stairway
leading to
roof terrace.

Guest
bedroom.

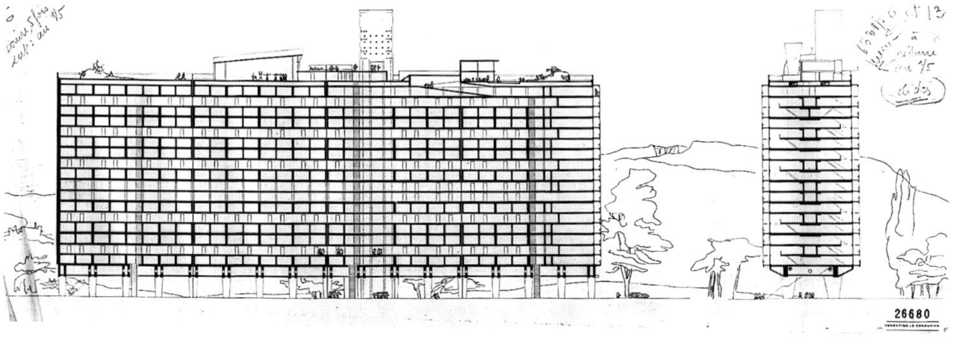


The Unité d'habitation of Marseilles was born as the result of the postwar urban reconstruction boom. It was supported by some important governmental figures throughout the successive unstable administrations and cabinets of the Fourth Republic in France.
In 1944, Raoul Dautry was appointed head of the Ministry of Urbanism and Reconstruction (MRU). A graduate of the prestigious École polytechnique, he had also headed the French railways and was Minister of Armaments (1939-1940). He also was interested in architecture and was a member of the social circle Le Corbusier maintained: the architect called on him in vain for the first time in 1936 about the interior furnishings for the cruise ship *L'Atlantique*; in January 1940, Dautry commissioned him for the cartridge factory of Aubusson in the Creuse region – called the "green factory," its foundations were partially built – and for about thirty portable lodging units for troops, also known as "Project Ham." The events of June 1940 stopped the works and contracts in progress. After the Liberation, Le Corbusier contacted Dautry again: Dautry then confirmed the town planning for Saint-Gaudens, Haute-Garonne, assigned to Le Corbusier's team, Lods and Cassan during the Occupation, and put him in charge of the reconstruction project in La Rochelle-La Pallice. None of these projects was to be completed, not even the program for Saint-Dié which was supported by industrialist Jean-Jacques Duval. Le Corbusier dreamed of the Seine, Perret got Le Havre. Marseilles was a consolation for Le Corbusier. The Unité was part of the experimental program ISAI, "buildings without individual allotments," financed by the French state, beginning in 1945, in order to deal with the housing crisis.

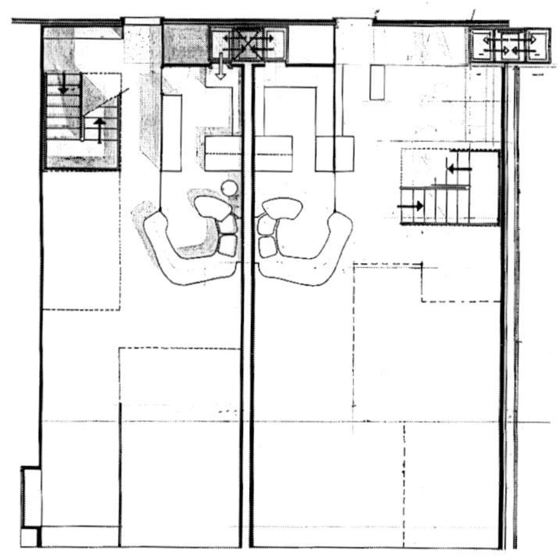

The Cité de Marseilles was exempted from the need for a building permit as well as from a certain number of regulations and obligations. It stretches out high (56 meters high by 135 meters long and 24 meters wide), echoing the "immeuble-villa" designed back in 1922 for the "pavillon suisse de la Cité universitaire de Paris" (based on the principle of the "bottlerack") and the Clarté building in Geneva (duplex apartments). The Unité was above all the first project entirely calculated using harmonic numbers, based on the human form: the Modulor. Hence its Corbusian name "unité d'habitation de grandeur conforme" (standard size housing unit). Thus, each unit is 3.66 meters wide by 2.26 meters high, the height in the living room rises to 4.84 meters (double height). Special attention was given to insulation, air conditioning and equipment exceptional for the era: the kitchen designed by Charlotte Perriand included an electric cooker, a refrigerator, active ventilation and an organic waste grinder. The *pilotis* were fitted with ducts that carried liquids and others that disposed of waste.
Construction was started in 1947 after hesitation over the plot and was completed five years later. In the process, the project received the firm support of another MRU minister, friend and champion of the architect, Eugène Claudius-Petit. Because of that friendship, after the election of Claudius-Petit as mayor in 1953, a little piece of the "ville radieuse" was erected in Firminy in the Loire region. Named Firminy-Vert, it included low-cost housing for 2,000 residents, cultural center and stadium (1955-1968), as well as an unfinished church.

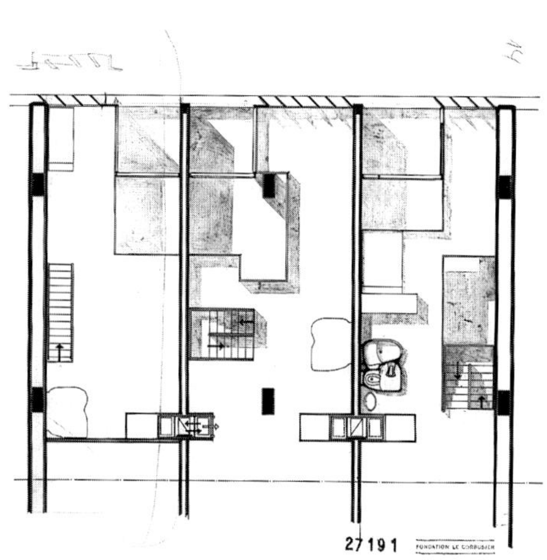


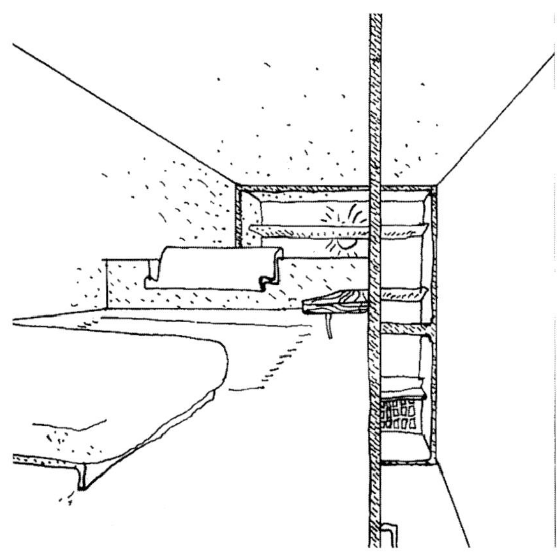

# Unité d'habitation, Marseilles

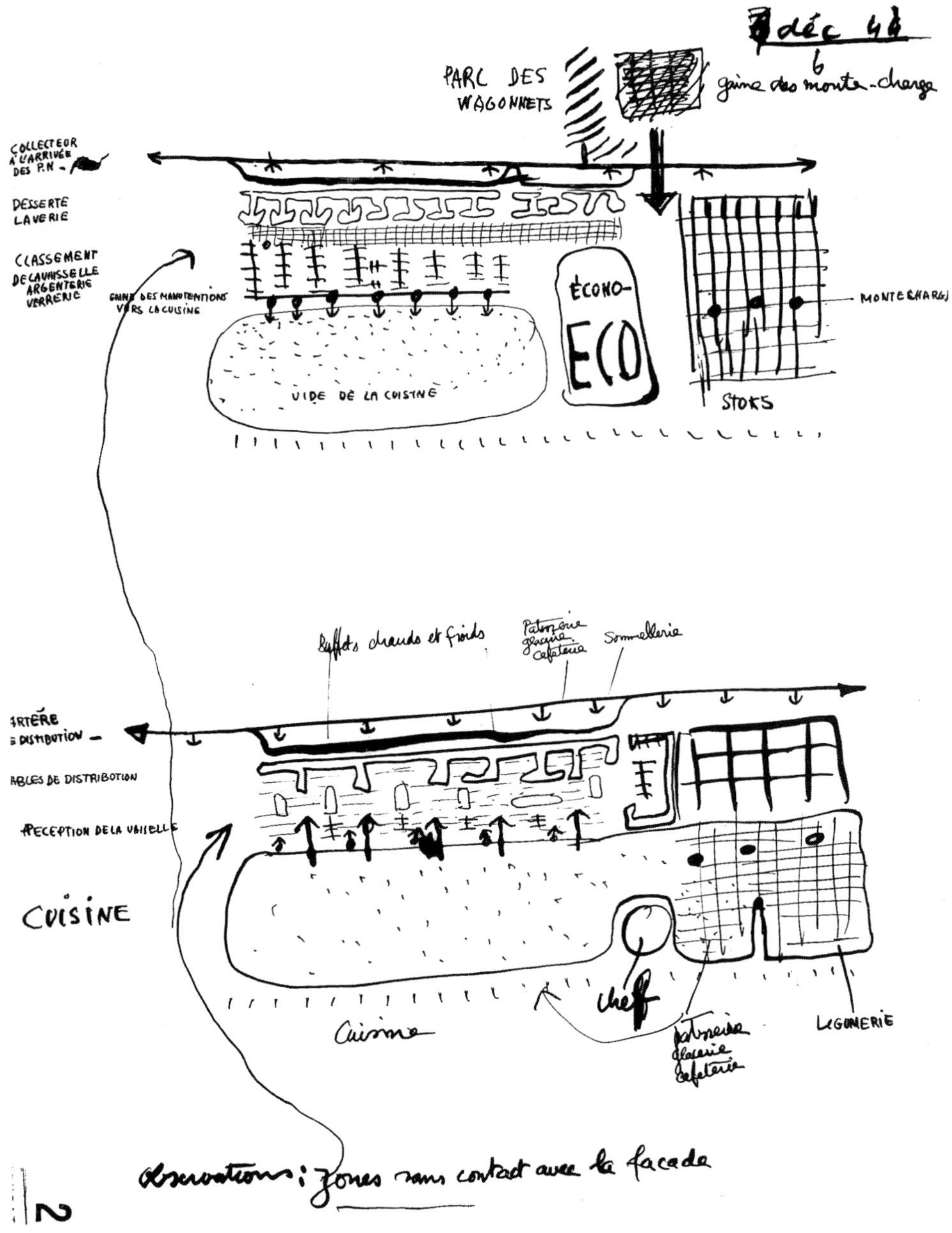


**Project architects:** Le Corbusier and his team the Atelier des bâtisseurs (ATBAT), directed by André Wogenscky (architecture division) and engineer Vladimir Bodiansky (technical studies division). With the contribution of Charlotte Perriand for the interior design.

**Client:** Ministry of Reconstruction and Urbanism (MRU), the initiative came from the Minister Raoul Dautry (1944-1946), who was followed in office by François Billoux, Claude Tillon, Jean Letourneau, René Coty and finally, for a longer period, by Eugène Claudius-Petit (1948-1952).

**Construction dates:** 1945-1952. The inauguration was held on the October 14, 1952, in the presence of Eugène Claudius-Petit.

**Description:** Eighteen-floor apartment building (330 duplex apartments in 23 different models), including interior streets and collective services (shopping street, hotel on the 7th and 8th floors, gymnasium, running track, theater and kindergarten on the roof).

**Location:** 280, boulevard Michelet, Marseilles, Bouches-du-Rhône, France.

**Current condition:** The Unité was sold one apartment after the other following its opening, becoming jointly owned in 1954. The hotel and the gymnasium are now privately run.

Internal street and access to shops.

*Opposite page:* Interior, view onto loggia balcony.

# Housing unit, radiant city: what wonderful slogans! What restorative formulas! But architectural enthusiasm is difficult to communicate: beyond words and outside the small circle of modern architects, the impressive Unité d'habitation (housing unit) in Marseilles did not enchant the natives. In the landscape – partly small houses, partly agricultural – of the time, it was an apparition which announced a new horizon of collective housing. The suburban imagination had a tough time accepting it.

To make it theirs, to guard themselves from its pretenses, and to respond to its formulas which snap like shibboleths, the inhabitants of Marseilles nicknamed it "la maison du fada" (*fada*: Marseilles slang for crazy).

The expression is not subtle, but it is not spiteful either. There is something of the house in the Unité d'habitation, something of the vertical and linear aggregation of houses, that lends a domestic scale to this complex of 348 apartments – not the least of its qualities. Madness also has a grip on the Cité radieuse (Radiant City). A visionary kind of madness, for the building still very much appears to be such a social and architectural innovator in the midst of the neighboring constructions which chose to remain dull. With its concrete hackles up, the Unité d'habitation shows itself best without any disguise: *pilotis* lifting up the body of the building in order to free up the ground arrangement, general compactness, animated roof terrace, double-height units, colorful loggias, integration of social premises and of shops, spacious glazed hall and so on. It is full of charms and Le Corbusier, vehement, but not "fada", endeavored to convince the authorities that he had developed solutions for collective housing that would make people happy and were intended to be reproduced.

Drawing inspiration from them did however turn out to be a problem in Nantes, Briey, Berlin and Firminy, Le Corbusier himself ran into financial difficulties and cultural reservations in order to reproduce his model in all its subtleties. Why did the idea not catch on? How is it that the heated debates brought on by the Cité radieuse had so little influence when the question of reconstructing the living environment of thousands of people in France arose? Why did the country not invest in this happy promise? Was it not sufficiently rich, educated and concerned with the common good? Did the country lack the enthusiasm necessary to believe in Le Corbusier's model?

In any case, the necessary conditions were not met to promote this model, and the Unité d'habitation in Marseilles remains an extravagance in the dully earnest world of French social housing.

In everything it puts forth, the Unité profoundly contravenes the spirit and the rules of this field.

The contraventions are as follows:
1. The Cité radieuse clearly demonstrates that social housing constitutes an opportunity rather than a fate solely reserved for the underclass, for people displaced after the war, for the jobbers of modernization, who must resign themselves to gaze at the bleak suburban cities sprung up in fields and be content with the meager consideration society grants these places.
It is said that this is regrettable, but inevitable.
What else could have been done? These housing projects were an answer to the urgency of the housing crisis and postwar poverty. They were progress compared to slums: the "common folk" benefitted.
Le Corbusier defended the opposite point of view: it is not possible to deal with a crisis or invoke its harshness in order to organize social relegation and then accept the ensuing cultural void. He asserted that architecture is always possible. He declared that social housing is architecture in full and constitutes a new culture. He warned that man's living environment would change drastically – to such an extent that it was indispensable that a total project, an ambitious community project, be thought out, going beyond the realm of pure economy, from the double angle of the utility and a diversified social content. The new housing conditions called for the design of new forms capable of nobly illustrating the importance of the task at hand. Le Corbusier worked on his building using a powerful aesthetic charge and carefully sketched out the smallest details of domestic life. That is the price to pay for harmony and, according to him, architecture cannot be qualified as social if all of these issues are not taken into consideration.
On that score, the Cité radieuse is, literally, an elaborate social construction, even if it does not meet the legal requirements for social housing. Living here, on this piece of land on the outskirts of Marseilles, and collectively experiencing a new organization in a suitable setting, is a lucky break to be seized upon.
2. The Cité radieuse provides evidence that collective housing, located on the fringe of the historic city, is not a makeshift for a middle class it is easy to think of as dreaming of quiet little houses or of apartments in an old town center, shaped by culture and rich sociability. The Unité d'habitation is much more than a transit zone in the backyard of the "real city." It is not a settlement for populations waiting for the social elevator. It is a city in itself, and shows no interest in the existing urban forms.
The Cité radieuse is a shower, a modern form of hygiene. It introduced an alternative culture and made a connection with a new vocabulary and imagination : the "green" city, constant sun, open space, dwellings

**Bedroom.**

***Opposite page:* Double-height living room and mezzanine.**

**Loggia**
**balcony.**

lengthened by loggias, light facades that open wide, easy driving conditions, the community run by itself, communal daycare facilities, sports facilities at the foot of the building, hydrotherapy and sun therapy spas on the terrace, gymnasiums in the building, integrated food supplies and so on.
Today, this vocabulary seems too ambitious: architects seem to be very cautious about social issues. They prefer not to go beyond the rules and regulations that define the economy and organization of social housing because the development of these criteria is beyond them. The formulas used by Le Corbusier have even more merit when they express joy in a subject that is joyous: social housing.
What can one currently say about our incapacity to qualify urban phenomena, apart from in the terms of a vocabulary that is abstract (towers, slabs, blocks, grids, cultural center, commercial center, sports center), administrative, (i.e., in France, ZUP, ZAC, ZEP, PLA, PLI), politically correct (mall, urban boulevard, centrality, urban court, town house) or cultural (citation, inscription, urban continuity, identity)? Where is the plan? What are the words? What do they mean?
Could it be that we have no positive words for life in social housing? That the subject has no more prospects? However, the very name "Cité radieuse" indicated clearly that housing and urban issues could mingle favorably.
3. The Cité radieuse is regulated by numbers although it is not an abstraction, neither displaying an accountant's mentality nor dully expressing repetition.
These numbers are: the Modulor, evidently, the "precise dimensions" of the living cell, the "exact size" also, and 1,200 people housed in 348 apartments on 18 floors, 56 meters high, 137 meters long and 24.4 meters wide. These figures constitute the critical mass of modernity. They allow for the establishment of the necessary conditions for a rich social life to blossom and transform the building into a little town, a city. Life, effectively maintained by these calculations, makes the dryness of numbers forgettable.
On the contrary, the soulless accounting of technocrats took over social housing during this period and controlled the figures that determined its contents, form and quality. The calculations were done by technicians who constantly tried to quantify, as exactly as possible, needs and comfort, to understand common practice, to define the essential outlines of the average resident – as, in other times, some ingeniously tried to weigh the soul. They succeeded in finding a result they immediately confined to a world of regulations. Of course, the figures which feed this beautiful machine are interspersed with opinion polls, corrected by

**Detail of niche in bedroom.**



***Opposite page:*** **Shopping street.**

the balance-sheets of managers, redirected by politicians, weighed according to the interests of the construction industry. Their complexity makes their very purpose vanish quickly : providing good housing for people. A magnificient abstraction sadly pervades. Collective housing, built using often obscure formulas and figures, became a field too serious to be turned over to architects whose calculations are far more pragmatic.
Le Corbusier enjoyed calculating, calculating dimensions, proportioning. But managing poverty in the same way as charity was organized was not his project. He did not see numbers as a punishment – quite the contrary – or as a means of extracting, by way of opinion polls, the magical substance: "what people want." His accounting was unusual: it enabled the organization of the surplus. The Unité d'habitation is generous: everything there seems to be a benefit, when in fact everything is adjusted and compact.
4. The Cité radieuse offers, in tight space, luxurious features and services. The good manager asks what people demand after they have acquired a taste for luxury? They will not go back, asserted Le Corbusier. The subtext: collective social housing, if it wanted to become widespread and ordinary, should seduce by offering new performances. Seduction? Performances?
Double orientation duplex apartments, equipped with balconies and deep loggias, adapted to different size families. They look so big. Soundproofed homes. Each door fitted with its own individual mailbox. Fitted kitchens containing a storage cupboard, an icebox (refrigerators were rare in 1952), a range hood and mechanical ventilation. A forced-air heating system and electric heaters were also provided as were ample closet space, a changing table, nooks, little shelves, carpentry, knobs – all meticulously designed.
The above are truly material assets, but it is more in terms of the mind that Le Corbusier produced his tour de force: he hid the label of inevitability that is stuck on social housing. The Cité radieuse is not a place of exile allotted in advance by an unkind destiny, it is a building that evokes mobility, travel, the horizon, the luxury of airplanes, boats, and grand hotels. There! In two strokes: first, the Unité d'habitation is endowed with an airy character. It is removed from the ground, and its multiple loggias are so many colored air pockets along the length of the facades. It seems ready to leave and one can imagine the residents bending out of their loggias, waving handkerchiefs, instead of drying laundry and fabric shades rolled down. The Unité d'habitation is like an outward bound cruise ship, a city on the go (soon the British would design cities on legs).

Second, the Unité d'habitation offered services reminiscent in many ways of those of a luxury hotel or transatlantic liner: a building for living is architecture plus services. Behind a proud canopy, a large, furnished lobby serves the apartments. A superintendent watches over the constant animation. Everyone passes through the lobby. There are personal messages posted, announcements for coming group activities. A battery of elevators takes one up – Le Corbusier planned for them to be operated by elevator attendants. Upstairs, the corridors are so big they are impressive: these are the "internal streets." They lead to a shopping mall, a daycare center for children, a sports center, a large terrace where parties are held. There was room service: one could use the intercom to order goods from the integrated shops, ice from the iceman, delivered to the storage cupboards or iceboxes. The social life of the building was organized, people chatted on the phone ever the more because it was free (the French telephone company put a stop to the intercom system since monopoly and equal access to public service require the smallest common denominator).

All of these arrangements were luxurious, and luxury is disturbing. Some find it corrupting while others suspect it to be disarming. Everyone agrees that it has no place in social housing (that is exactly where its interest lies). It is common sense, to those who find luxury corrupting, to know that it is not society's mission to offer luxury to the poor. The calculations of those who find luxury disarming demand that nothing is to be expected from that society. The Cité radieuse is completely extravagant and far too expensive, they complained.

Too expensive in relation to what? Where are the figures? Who calculated the maximum price of social housing with no concern for urban planning or including the predictable social deficits that we have been paying for years. Was Le Corbusier wrong when he quoted figures and stated he knew the right price for the solution of the problem at hand: happily building, outside of the traditional city, lively mass housing? Today the Unité d'habitation in Marseilles is buzzing with animation and was not built at a loss. It remains a capital asset: it has become a private property owned by its residents.

Le Corbusier did not respect the regulations of social housing: one imagines him as moody and seeking to impose his strong talent. While admiring him, one keeps him out of this field as it is, so it is said, an exercise of humility. That is going too fast. He did not submit to these regulations because he judged the conditions that they established insufficient. He thought that the architect's first duty was to force these rules and to go beyond circumstances when they are not reasonable. Very few followed him on that path. L'Atelier de Montrouge and Jean

**Roof terrace.**

***Opposite page:*** **Entrance canopy.**

**Entrance pavilion.**

**Circulation between *pilotis*.**

Roof terrace.

Detail of the stained-glass piece representing the Modulor.

*Opposite page:* Entrance pavilion and the Modulor stained-glass piece.

*Following pages*: Facade on boulevard Michelet.

Nouvel, for example, are worth mentioning.

After the war, the imperatives concerning the rebuilding and modernization of France required massive construction to accommodate many people. Most architects and urbanists were not ready, whether intellectually or technically, to take on such a challenge. On the contrary, from the 30s onward, these problems were the core of the preoccupations of Le Corbusier and other modern architects. When history would eventually call on them, they would have little opportunity to use their skills and put their thinking into practice. However, when a scapegoat for the ensuing urban disaster is sought, it is the name of Le Corbusier that comes up first.

This is both unfair and paradoxical: one cannot blame Le Corbusier for having been a bad inspiration of what he did not carry out when what he did do in Marseilles is a success that inspired no one.

DEMENA

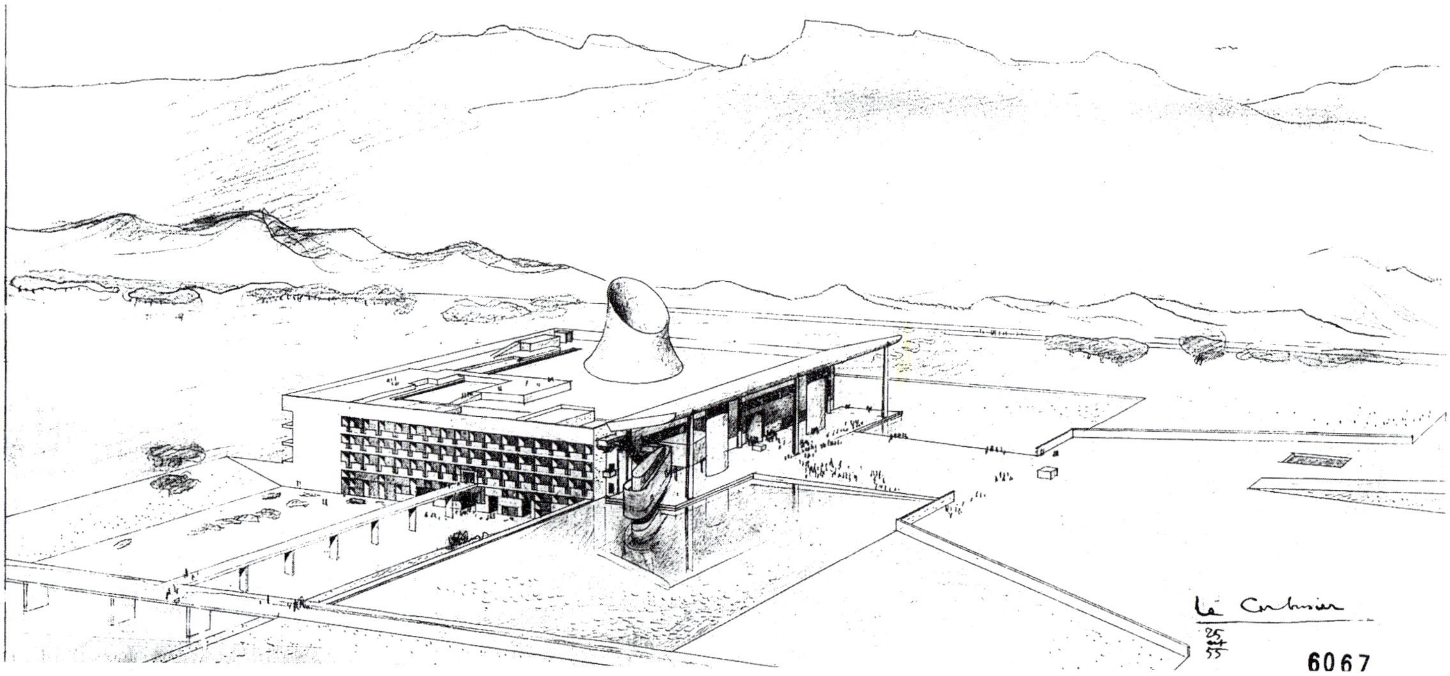


110

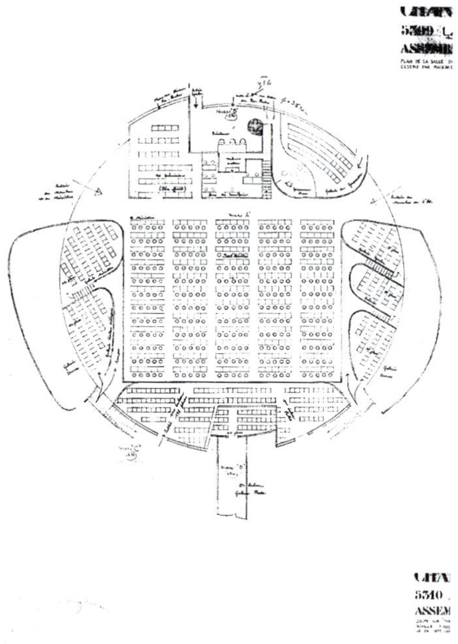

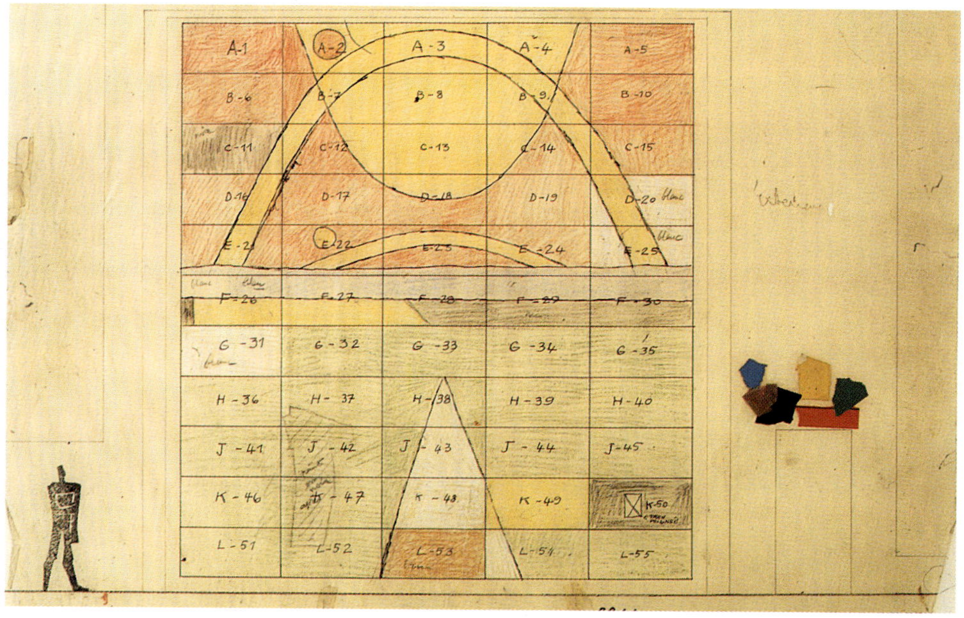

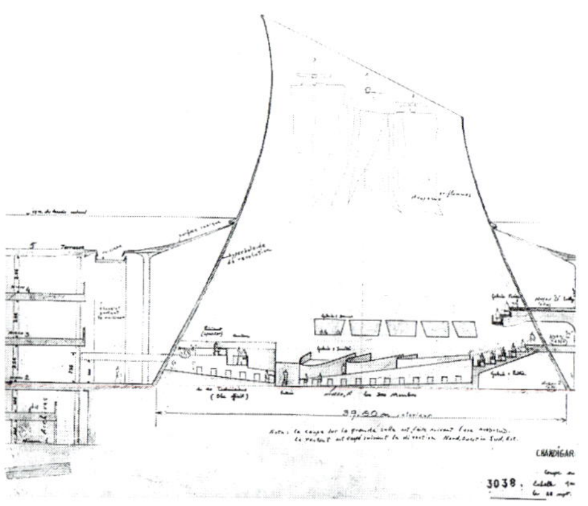

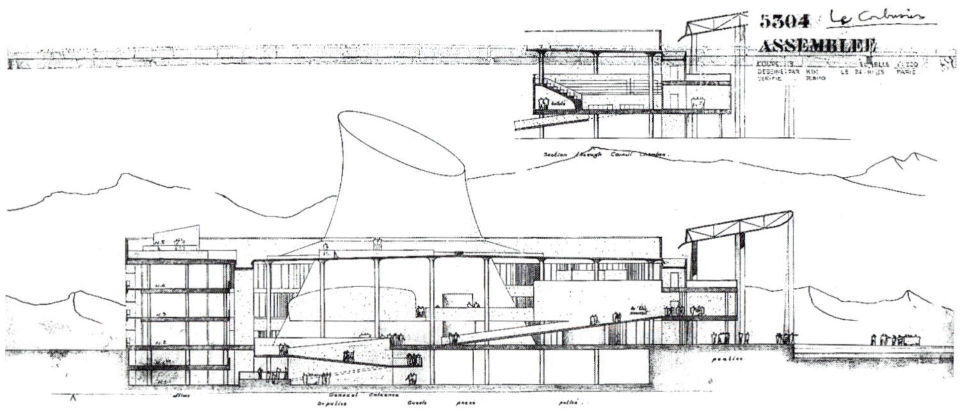


*Plans and drawings for the Assembly.*

# Capitol, Chandigarh

*Drawings of the Secretariat.*



**Project architects:** Le Corbusier with the contribution of Pierre Jeanneret, Jane Drew and Maxwell Fry. Le Corbusier also created the monumental tapestries and the ceremonial doors of the Parliament (in enameled sheet-iron) given by France to the State of Punjab in 1964.

**Client:** State of Punjab, India.

**Construction dates:** 1951-1962.

**Description:** Complex of public buildings where the executive powers (Secretariat, 1958), the legislative powers (Palace of Assembly, 1962, inaugurated in 1964) and legal authorities (High Court, 1955) of the State of Punjab are located.

**Location:** Chandigarh, territory of the Indian Union, political and administrative capital of the States of Punjab and (since 1967) of Haryana, located in northwestern India, at the foot of the Himalayas. The Capitol makes up the northernmost point of the city.

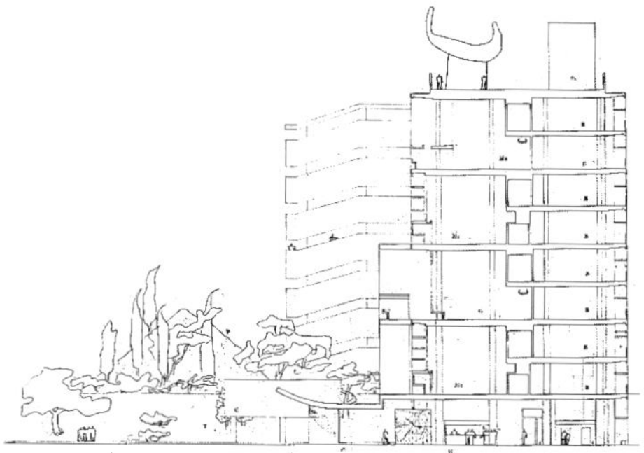

In 1947, independent India turned over the western part of Punjab to Pakistan, including the old provincial capital, Lahore. The site for a new capital at the foot of the Himalayas was chosen in 1948 by P. L. Varma, chief engineer of Punjab and P. N. Thapar, director of public works. At Nehru's request, the master plan of Chandigarh was assigned to American Albert Mayer, who worked on it from 1949 to 1950. In December 1950, after Mayer's closest assistant's death, the Indian authorities put together a new team that was European. Spring 1951 saw four CIAM architects meet there to shape Chandigarh : Le Corbusier, who was appointed general consultant, Pierre Jeanneret (the city's chief architect until 1965), Jane Drew and Maxwell Fry (on location for three years). Apart from the plan, Le Corbusier let his colleagues set up an in situ workshop and work on the various parts and the housing prototypes. He devoted himself to the complex of public buildings that constitute the Capitol, backed up by his Paris workshop for the drawings and the studies.

Although the layout of Chandigarh was co-signed by Mayer, for the first time after numerous set-backs – Rio (1938), Algiers (1942), Saint-Dié (1945), La Rochelle (1946), Bogota (1950) – Le Corbusier finally saw his principles for the "organization" of the city materialize, drawing on the lines of his *Ville radieuse,* minus the skyscrapers. Construction in Chandigarh started in 1951, the year after the Indian Constitution was promulgated. The site particularly interested Nehru who personally supervised the birth of this "temple of the new India."

Situated at the north end of the city, on the main artery Jan Marg, the Capitol is made up of three public buildings: the palaces of the Assembly and the High Court, and the Secretariat which includes seven ministries and their various services.

The original program included a fourth element, the Governor's palace, which remained just a frame (1951-1954). In Chandigarh (and Ahmedabad), Le Corbusier gathered the elements of what historian William J. R. Curtis calls his "Indian grammar." The symbol of the crescent is ever present (the bull's horns of his *Carnets*) in the architect's world. He had intended to fit a certain number of symbol-monuments into the composition of the Capitol : an S shape depicting sunrise and sunset in front of the "fosse de la Considération," a "tower of Shadows" as a celebration of the Modulor, the monumental sculpture "La Main ouverte," and so forth. The first sketch of that steel emblem dates back to 1951; it was finalized in 1964 and finished in 1985.

Le Corbusier designed other intra muros projects as well as projects for the surroundings, some of which saw the light of day: a school of art and architecture (1964-1969), a museum and art gallery (1964-1968) and a yachting club on the shores of the artificial lake Sukhna. Others, such as the 1952 sketches for a "peasant" house, did not materialize.

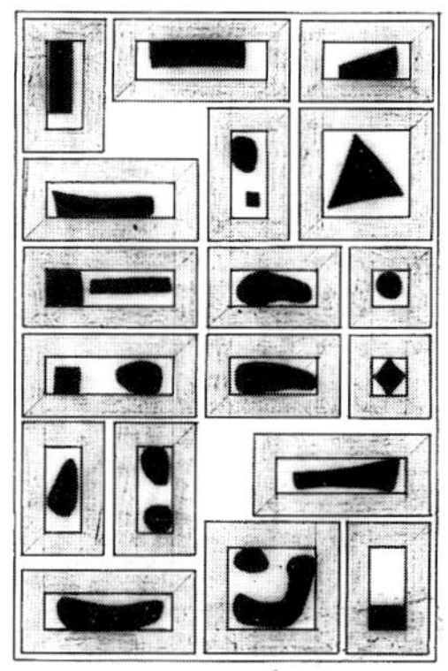

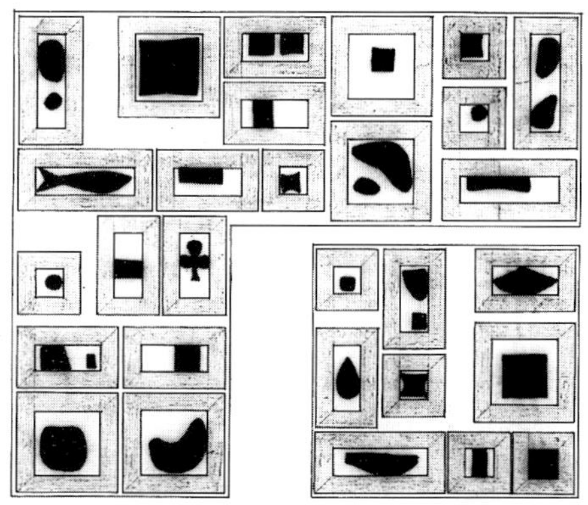

*View of the Secretariat and drawings for the High Court.*

*Le Corbusier in Chandigarh (1955).*

"The Open Hand."

Assembly and square.

*Opposite page:* **Southwestern corner of the Assembly.**



In 1947, India won its independence and soon thereafter Pakistan was created from part of its territory. Much blood was spilt in the process. Pakistan became a Muslim state, the new India gave itself democratic institutions, chose to be a non-aligned country and attracted the world's sympathy. Nehru, its first Prime Minister, decided to build a new capital, Chandigarh, for the state of Punjab, traumatized by the loss of its major cities. Wished for by a democracy looking for its bearings in a country held back by a caste system, this city would offer the opportunity to portray the recent political ties binding the people and their representatives. Democracy, striving to make all things equal, tends to take the drama out of human relationships. By establishing laws that apply to all, the democratic state deals with conflicts, corrects excess, separates good from bad. Individual morality no longer needs to feed on exemplary feats of virtue: what modern society authorizes is not deemed bad. In an established democracy, the heroes are sportsmen, singers or gentle people. Legendary heroes are bored there.

Under this type of regime, the actions of the most enterprising men are aimed toward trade or technology and their most remarkable accomplishment is not serving as a moral example later. The engineer and the industrialist, the elite to which Le Corbusier often paid tribute endlessly think up and disseminate objects that are amoral. On the other hand, when they are powerfully attractive, these objects can deflect passions from moral considerations by directing them toward the ambiguous realm of taste for technical performances. Le Corbusier crossed that blurred line in 1935, in a book where he explains his fascination for airplanes and praises wars for developing aviation technology. This consideration would be unimportant if it were not for the fact that Le Corbusier drew most of the moral and aesthetic arguments for his architecture from the world of machines.

Le Corbusier was a moralist as well as a man of action who was particularly enterprising. Although his world was focused on exemplary objects – airplanes, boats, industrial products – it was also strongly influenced by pure ideas that transcended his attraction to brute force. These ideas had moral connotations in so much as they reinvented, outside academic dogma, the architect's rules of conduct. They make a distinction between what is fair, useful and beautiful and what is false, useless and vulgar.

The first of the great Corbusian principles is that the world must renew itself by leaning on regulating forces if it wants to avoid social revolution, regression and decadence. At that time, modern society did not have many of these forces. They could be found in the regulating effects

expressed by the rational thinking of engineers and industrialists. Le Corbusier praised the "exactness" of this technical intelligence which fed his theories on architectural standards and mass production. The regulating forces were also produced by the powerful ideological and political systems which attracted a fair share of Europe during the first third of the century. Communism, Nazism, Fascism, Francoism, which Le Corbusier, usually so easily outraged, seemed to put up with, as he did not react when the Bauhaus was closed, quoted Mussolini and approached the Pétain administration in Vichy.

Le Corbusier's will was strong. He wanted to transform the world radically according to a plan that was both rational and spiritual. This plan needed the support of the authorities of the time and did not let itself be rebuffed, when the occasion arose, by the order those powers maintained or by the ideas they propagated. Le Corbusier placed his architecture beyond the realm of politics and considered it a factor of order favorable to "rational thought" and, therefore, to his projects.

The second of the great Corbusian principles – the new society, appropriately organized, will find its spiritual balance if it may refer to exemplary representations which express the harmony of mind and spirit as well as that of the present and history. Architecture, because it is capable of powerfully making this synthesis, offers new reasons for joy to the man whom the furor of the modern world has torn away from its traditional hierarchies, its habitual representations, its body of legends.



**Two views of the Assembly, eastern facade.**

Le Corbusier thus strove to compose works which convey a feeling of "spiritual unity." It was up to these works to fill the void left by the ebbing of spiritual beliefs and enchantments. This gap is not successfully filled by money – Le Corbusier called it "Americanism" – or the machine despite their fury and all the objects they throw at it. Hence, by working without fail on the material provided by the world's fascinating and terrible triviality, Le Corbusier sought to reveal that a higher meaning could be bestowed upon the collective effort to produce.

The rough energy which crosses the collective push forward – all the more effective when it is organized – will happily transform itself into a spiritual principle if it finds it possible to consume itself in a work of art. The creator, the architect in this case – freed of all constraints or indoctrination, alone – is the author of this transformation. It is the individual act of creation that gives mechanistic and commercial society its depth and mystery.

To remain in step with a troubled era in which tensions flare up quickly and the performance of machines is overwhelming, Le Corbusier tried to impress, to move people with his lyricism by representing the

"architectural drama." The building guides the passions and turns them into a spectacle whose moral argument stems from the fact that both the roads to authenticity and to transcendency are expressed in it.
The architectural spectacle is real if it knows how to change the "exact" technical, economic and sociological reality, into a convincing spiritual work that is capable of arousing emotion. Le Corbusier had a formula: "Technique is the very seat of lyricism," and one conviction: technique does not lie. Architecture lifts the spirit of the era if, through pathos, it transforms modern reality. It is easy to follow Le Corbusier when he explains how the new conditions of the modern world, its new materials – concrete, steel, plate glass – result in a new aesthetics, inspire visions of a happy future and allow for new ways of using things. One understands "modernity": that is, the soundness and the lyricism of its white villas, rational apartment buildings and radically clear urban planning.
The spectacular shape of his architecture, whose lyricism is still surprising, cannot be dissociated from his brusque argumentation. They are the two sides to the modernity that Le Corbusier stubbornly tried to establish. He was prepared, in his desire to correspond to reality, to incorporate a surrealistic kind of humor. "There is architecture in the telephone and in the Parthenon," dared to say the man who was overwhelmed by the Acropolis. Is there architecture on the Internet and in Ronchamp?
Thanks to this spectacle seeking to inspire transcendence, Le Corbusier carefully maintained the part of the absolute that architecture knew how to tackle throughout its history. He also continued exploring the routes to higher order: the expression of the sacred, the relationship to the forces of nature, the manifestation of the temporal power, divested of any form of ideology. But, as far as architectural transcendence was concerned, the world proved to be recalcitrant. The world is known to be materialistic and disenchanted; the new powers, having divided the world between themselves, did not find their bearings in modern architecture. Le Corbusier knew this from bitter experience with the Soviets, the League of Nations and the United Nations.
Thus, our architect, as hero, would force the world; as a true artist, he would create the conditions for his intervention; as a moralist, he would erect his own edifying theater. One admires him and one understands that, seeking intangible harmonies, he made too much use of lessons on controlling lines, elementary geometry and the Modulor as generator of order. One understands that he enlisted the Sun in his revolution as well as nature and geography, whether laying out cities or the smallest of human habitations. One understands also why he courted power in all its forms. But, as one gets the feeling that such a solitary enterprise

**Ceremonial door of the Assembly. Enamelwork by Le Corbusier.**

Opposite page: Southeastern facade of the Secretariat.

Secretariat, southeastern facade.

Passage underneath the Secretariat.

is desperate, it is not surprising that our hero, in Chandigarh, ran into the problem of representing the sacred: he rushed into it and got lost because of excessive enthusiasm. On one hand, he confused divinity and artistic creativity. On the other hand, as he saw God everywhere and nowhere, he seized a large temporal subject – a capital for Indian democracy – and transformed it into a hieratic liturgy, full of overwhelming mystery.

When Le Corbusier arrived in India, he was convinced of his own genius. He spoke of himself in the third person. Architecture was his medium. In Chandigarh, Le Corbusier found ideal operating conditions that heightened the exalted atmosphere he tended to move in. Nehru, a leader carried by history, was his interlocutor. He saw nonaligned India as an India not blinded by mercantile or collectivist ideologies. He thought that India, more than any other nation, would recognize the profoundly fair quality of his modern architecture and would discover what "the eyes that do not see" refused to consider back in the West. He imagined that this India, peopled by gods, would be immediately sensitive to the spiritual part of his work. India, as the "millenarian civilization" unpolluted by materialistic thinking, would offer a unique opportunity to connect the immemorial past to the purest of present times. He was convinced that India, where innumerable and enduring crowds lived, would know how to cover uncomplainingly the never-ending promenades he had in mind.



One does not wonder for long about the reason behind the endless distances running through Chandigarh. Their purpose is to draw a clear line between the Capitol – the representative, administrative and legislative functions – and the city itself and its residents. There is a distinction made between those you wield power and the others; the head is separated from the body. The debaters, decision makers, judges and administrators at work are sheltered from interminable avenues that function like walls less high than those of the Kremlin or the Forbidden City, but just as effective at expressing absolute power, how it goes unpunished, and the fear it wishes to inspire. The dimensions of Chandigarh are frightful, and this frightfulness is maintained by the buildings of the Capitol. Their aesthetic strength, admirable in itself, and the pathos they express, make a misleading arrangement which, placed in a space stretched out to the point of being absurd, establishes the mystery of their presence by making ours seem incongruous.

Everything was calculated so that a supreme power, impossible to grasp and difficult to express, impressed man as much as possible. To him, the Capitol seemed a taboo place. Within this enclosure, full of strange things he imagines to be sacred, not spotting the eye of a

THE HARYANA STATE COOP. APEX BANK LTD.

God overlooking it, he finds no intercessor except Le Corbusier himself. His pre-eminence being confirmed by the fact that, in four days, he drew the plans of a city for 150,000 residents, like He who took six to create the world. On the fifth day – and for years thereafter – Le Corbusier sought the absolute. He began drawing the Capitol, residence of the local half-gods, Olympus at the foot of the Himalayas. But the Greek gods are more terrifying, funnier and profound than Indian officials. The whole thing has a sad effect, democratic representation is canceled; nothing has been announced regarding it. The seats of elective power are smuggled out of the site which is, however, the only possible theater for democracy. In this theater, the citizens are the audience as well as the actors. They pay to see, hear and enforce their judgement. The Capitol of Chandigarh, full of a drama whose arguments it is impossible to grasp, whose greatness acts to the extent of destabilizing, is conceived like a representation of the sacred. Le Corbusier is the only hero on that empty and mute stage that refers only to his deeds. Today, those who seek to prolong the performance forget that this production was staged for the sole benefit of the master and the audience is not in the theater.

Nonetheless, the architecture of the Capitol is magnificent. The Court of Justice, the Assembly, the Secretariat are works of genius. Without

**High Court, northwestern facade.**

***Opposite page:*** **Lawyers' quarter, southeastern facade.**



***Following pages:*** **"Brise-soleil".**

**Access ramps leading to the floors and oval oculus.**



***Following pages:*** **High Court.**

***Underneath and opposite page:*** **Northwestern facade.**

doubt, there nobleness comes from the fact they were born into it and from their dimensions. They are born – here and now, very large – of the operation of the most free and most vivid aesthetic inventiveness. Before, there was nothing like them; now, their dignity leaves one baffled. Here, architecture finds an importance that no other city could grant. At the Capitol, the Corbusian machine goes full blast. But, in Chandigarh, the first motor of Corbusian thought – exactness and beauty are rooted in reality – is broken. Thus, the motor was only a secondary mechanism.

What is essential is transformation and transmutation. That is the work of the artist, his duty. Reality is only a material – iron, concrete, airplanes, cars or cruise ships – the whole modern mechanism only serves to feed the chemistry of creation. These are the elements, among others, of transmutation. Only Le Corbusier's powerful mind and cerebral energy could serve as examples for the Indian masses. Unplugged from any source of energy produced by machine or designed by engineers, his thinking ran wild. Nothing at Chandigarh is a redefinition of reality: thus, nothing is radically modern.

So what if democracy is embarrassed placed in an awkward situation by bellicose heroes? The time for Corbusian architecture is eternity. Modernity is a means, not a dogma : Le Corbusier did not use hewn stone, marble and the orders, because that had already been done – the transformation had already taken place a long time ago in Greece. The drama was acted by the heroes of antiquity, the best, and Le Corbusier was on friendly terms with them.

His architecture is a theater. The aesthetic power of his work is less intended to flatter the art lover than to impress by the example of its greatness and strangeness. It wants to make an impression so as to reform the tendencies – to doubt, to let go, to be disorderly and irrational – it notices in society. This theater expresses drama through space, through the manipulation of excess space: that is, flatly taken into consideration, through the organization of the excess void. The Corbusian void was essential in the expression of his power, his magic, of the power of magic. This void is huge in Chandigarh. It is even larger as Le Corbusier's stage was completely out of tune with the tragic dimensions of the first half of a century, when the civilized world bet all it had, with results that incited the bleakest pessimism and that only the active representation of an open democracy could expiate.

CHK 4949

PB28
9512

NIPPO
CHE
6032
CH-OIF
2448
PB-65 6261

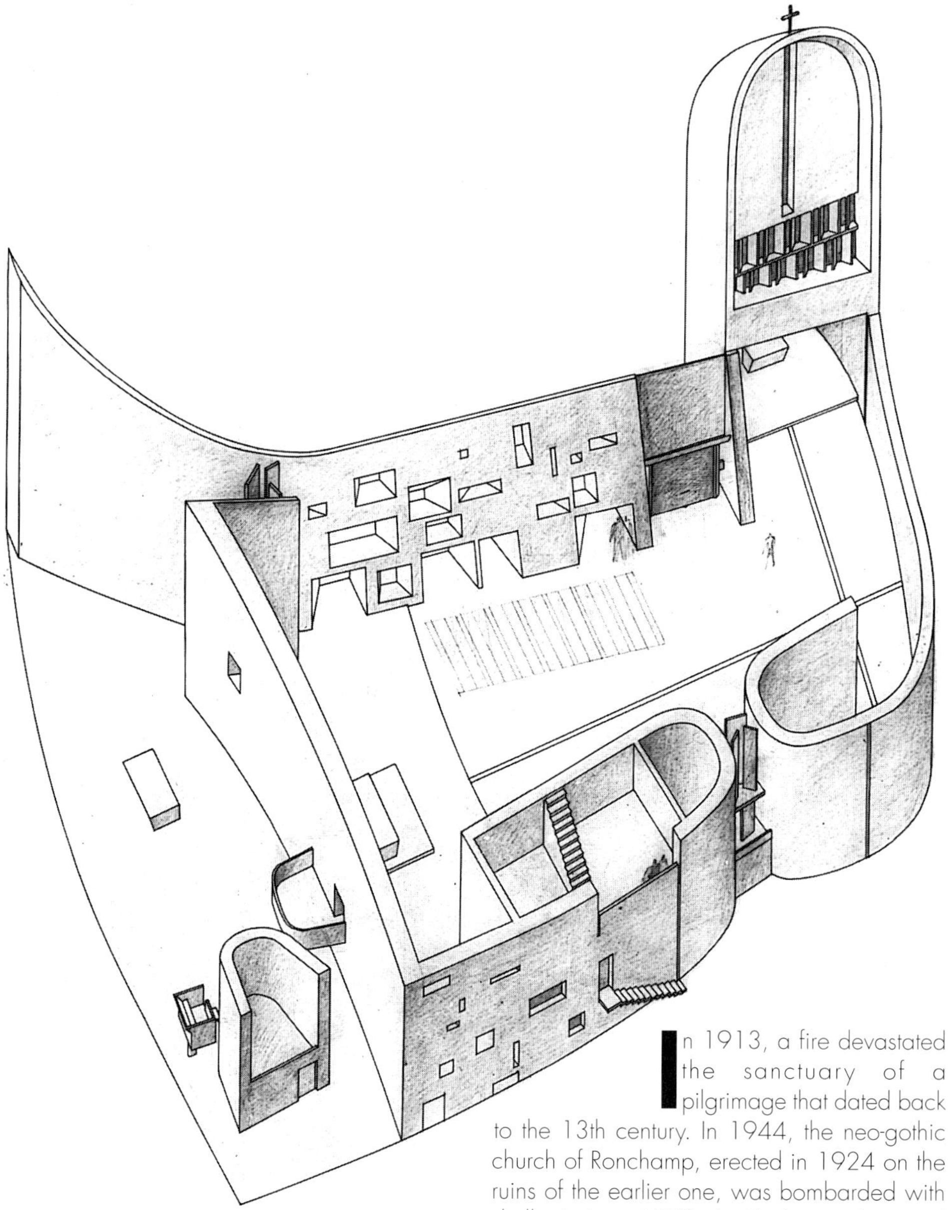

In 1913, a fire devastated the sanctuary of a pilgrimage that dated back to the 13th century. In 1944, the neo-gothic church of Ronchamp, erected in 1924 on the ruins of the earlier one, was bombarded with shells. In June 1950, Le Corbusier designed the round forms of Notre-Dame-du-Haut, topped by a roof shaped like a crab-shell. André Maisonnier made the initial model submitted to the diocese.

The project for the chapel of Ronchamp was part of the renewal of sacred architecture, at the heart of the religious reconstruction program of the postwar years desired by the Church and supported by some clergymen, including Father Couturier and Father Régamey. The chapel was also implicated in the discussion about the intrusion of modernity in places of worship: Ronchamp ignored the ugly quarrel going on about the sculptures and stained glass windows of Rouault, Lurçat, Léger, Matisse and others, to superbly capture thoughts on space and light. Initiative for the project came from Canon Lucien Ledeur, secretary of the diocesan board of Sacred Art in Besançon, and François Mathey, also a member of the board, both admirers of the architect. Le Corbusier was not the first architect to be consulted on the project (Jean-Charles Moreux headed an earlier project that ended up being abandoned). He received the appreciative and fervent support of Father Couturier, director of the magazine *L'Art sacré*, and member of the *L'Architecture d'aujourd'hui* board: "We considered Le Corbusier not only the greatest living architect, but also the architect with the most authentic and strongest spontaneous awareness of the sacred." The works of Le Corbusier include plans for five religious buildings: the church of Tremblay-en-France (1929, with Pierre Jeanneret, never built), the basilica and "cité de contemplation" of La Sainte-Baume (1945-1951, with Edouard Trouin, never built), the chapel Notre-Dame-du-Haut (1950-1955), the monastery of la Tourette (1950-1960, with a collegiate team of architects and engineers) and the church Saint-Pierre de Firminy (1960, with José Oubrerie, unfinished).



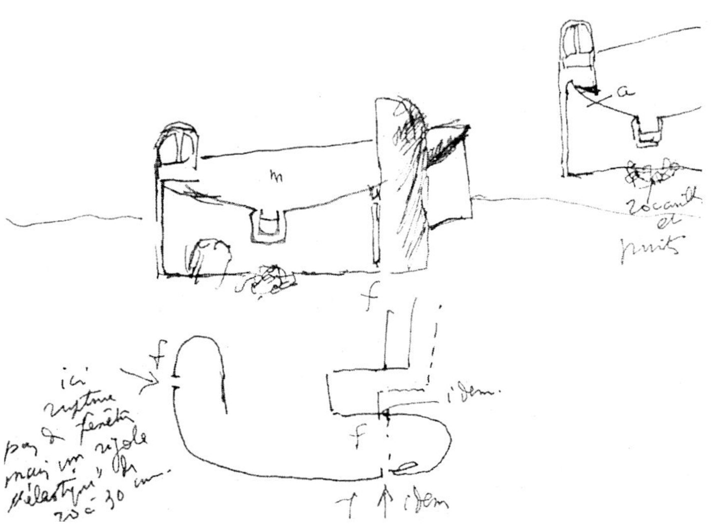

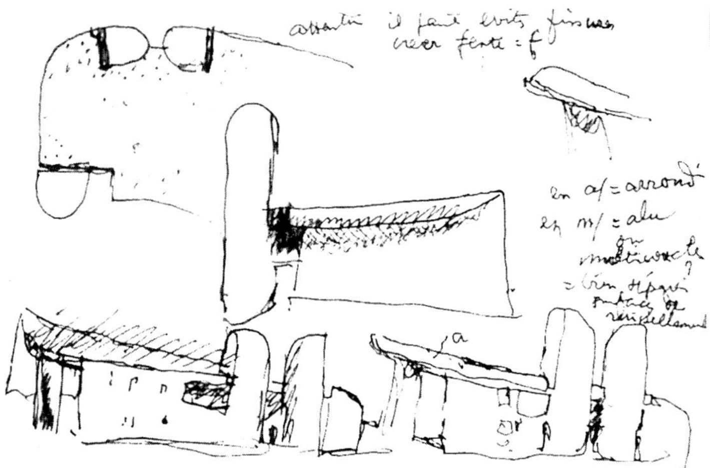

# Chapel of Notre-Dame-du-Haut

**Project architect:** Le Corbusier.

**Invited artist:** Joseph Savina (benches, Cross). Enamel works by Ateliers Jean Martin in Luynes, France. *Vierge à l'Enfant,* 17th-century polychrome wooden sculpture.

**Client:** Société immobilière of Notre-Dame-du-Haut, with the diocesan board of Sacred Art of the city of Besançon, France.

**Construction dates:** 1950-1955.

**Description:** Reconstruction of a pilgrim's chapel, dedicated to the Marian cult.

**Location:** Ronchamp, Haute-Saône, on the hill of Bourlémont, route de Belfort, Lure, France.

Up on the hill, stands something immediately sensual although it resembles nothing known and its size is impressive. This large upheaval of shapes that seem to be giving way is truly overwhelming and it is difficult to find words to describe it. So, to steady the way up the little steep path leading to the building, one mentally holds on to the commonplace that Le Corbusier, drawing inspiration from the beautiful landscape and the higher quality of the subject – a chapel dedicated to the Virgin Mary – turned out an incredibly lyrical work, a real sculpture. A brilliant architect and sculptor, he demonstrates the full range of his talent here. Happy to act the art lover, one gazes at the building from a distance and adjusts to what the myth of the artist supposes of irrationality, bizarreness and, in the end, foreignness. Thus, sure of having gained some enlightenment and having filled up on superlative adjectives, one hurries back because of the cold.

There is nothing foreign about Ronchamp. It is an invitation, one can rub against it, grab it as if it were a flexible fabric, bring it close to the body. It is a warm – the warmth of the body – and comfortable building. But this is not a given. One does not warm immediately to such a singular creation as it is not uniquely sensual. It is even more true because its mental aspect is difficult to comprehend, unlike other works by Le Corbusier that are introduced by a solid theoretical apparatus. Does one wish to talk about the chapel or simply try to describe it? It can be touched upon lightly, but one should not count on being able to find the words to define it. This building entails an infinite amount of liberty.

There is no choice but to accept that to talk about Ronchamp is to talk about oneself. This is about sharing one's own experience of that chapel. It is the viewer who invents Ronchamp.

One has visited many chapels dedicated to the Virgin. The most moving ones are the result of pure and simple architecture. This is not the case here; nothing gives Ronchamp away as a Marian place of worship. Lyrical shapes in the image of religious sentiment? Yes, but they are rough and fashioned from a lumpy material. At first glance, the shapes express an uncultivated spirituality, like new, seeking to be expressed and seeming to originate in the freshly converted local pagan cults. These shapes evoke the statuettes of animist deities that go back to the earliest worship of pot-bellied idols. One thinks of a well-fed mother goddess figure, at once terrifying and comforting. Beset upon by the dark forest, wedged under an immense sky full of magical powers, one lets oneself be fascinated by imagining oneself in the heart of darkness.

This is the wrong track. The air is pure. The chapel is white and its shapes

**Eastern facade.**

***Opposite page:* Southern facade.**

***Previous pages:* Aerial view of Notre-Dame-du-Haut.**

seem to send out an invitation. This is a place of fervent pilgrimage, dedicated to the Virgin Mary, dating back a long time. The bells ring and the quiet crowd kneels down.

But where is the Virgin? She is an essential figure. The Catholic Church chose, in order to propagate, to represent its fundamental belief – the Incarnation of Christ, He who carries the word of God – in which the Virgin plays her role. Where is her image? There is a little polychrome sculpture, modestly set in a niche carved in the wall: it is a secondary element in the architectural composition. And where is the Cross, another essential component of the Incarnation? Of course, one does not expect to come upon it in the layout of the chapel. But one spots a puny one on top of one of the buildings. Then one sees two other ones on the ground. Their value results as much from their impact in terms of art as from their symbolic importance. This is perfect, but the ensuing effect is complex, whereas the church traditionally uses clear and hierarchical compositions. Where are the saints, the martyrs and the images of religious history? They are not here and it is better that way. The chapel is relieved from the problem of representation in which the Catholic Church has been entangled for so long, making due with mediocre imagery, oozing blood at best, made even more sickening by the smell of incense, as if seeking further mortification. Le Corbusier does not offer a literal representation of his subject matter. One can only be thankful: his pictorial composition on the door of the chapel is not convincing and when he inscribes "Hail Mary" in falsely naive handwriting on a stained glass window, the result requires indulgence. Ronchamp expresses something far more powerful without resorting to images. The chapel is not an abstract creation: the building takes on representation to the point of making the Catholic faith tangible.

The very bodies of the pilgrims are imprinted on the chapel. Its design is subtle compared to the didactic layout of the "architectural promenades" – invented by Le Corbusier – that blends the linear movement of bodies and architectural composition. In Ronchamp, nothing is rectilinear or defined. A kind of Brownian movement saturates the entire space and produces a field where the pilgrims' trail appears. This very field is generated by a series of autonomous objects staged both inside and outside. Each object captures a gesture from the liturgy. They are scattered about without any hierarchical order, all over, according to what appears to be a lucky chance. Although these objects are detached from each other, they do correspond with one another as part of a network: a blurred line, a wave, joins each of them. A hazy design is shaped, signalling the stations of the believer and transfixing his ritual gestures.

**Northwestern corner.**

**Northern facade.**

***Opposite page:* Eastern facade with altar and pulpit.**

The worshipper prays, kneeling or sitting on these elaborate polished benches placed on a slanted base. On the side, he prostrates himself along a pleated steel shape. A bit further, he makes his confession hidden in a concrete cube. Elsewhere, he crosses himself with holy water drawn from boxes that are like pivots. Mass is celebrated behind altars made of stone blocks set on the ground which gives way in places, as if it were sagging under the weight of the pilgrims. The sermon is preached from structures directed toward the sky. Enigmatic stairs lead up to them. All of these elements hold the rank of objects and, as each of them bears the imprint of the believers or the clergy: they all harmonize with one another to produce a resonance.
This vibration is intimately contained by the chapel's walls, exactly suited to the fervor of the small crowd. The interior, all curves and pleats, is like a piece of clothing that is just loose enough to allow one to place oneself somewhere that is both closely fitted and immensely vast: yet another space, but celestial and dilated by faith. A womb that is to the crowd at Ronchamp what a crab shell, one of Le Corbusier's inspirations for this work, is to the crustacean: a precise envelope for the flesh that speaks of the infinity of nature. This envelope is warmer than the immense vaults of cathedrals and more luminous than the thick walls of Romanesque chapels. Thus, it is a womb, a belly, represented by the swelling of the concrete veils. It is no less than the Virgin's belly. Ronchamp shows the point where nature and the divine mingle.
A scene painted by Piero della Francesca comes to mind: the Virgin points out her rounded stomach emerging from layers of fabric that shape curves, points and pleats. She stares at the spectator, not with the look of a timid young girl, but with that of a woman who knows the cause as well as the effects and knowingly endures it all. Is it the look of a creator? No doubt. But then, when one is standing in front of Ronchamp, is it not the gaze of Le Corbusier one experiences? On the contrary, nothing is compulsory. One remains alone, almost powerless in the face of the work's mystery: the creator – that is, the architect – may be everywhere, but is also nowhere at the same time. He knew how to efface himself before his subject matter, to disappear behind the object; he is weightless, even though his trail is immense.
The building is composed of so many different materials and follows so many seams that it appears not to have been made by a single creator. Instead, one imagines the pilgrims, over the years, resuming construction and enhancing it by a series of donations, the many parts of the chapel are like offerings.
Here, time decides, and because of its work, the chapel ensures its own stunning presence as much as it integrates its own ruin.

***Opposite page:*** **Western facade, detail.**

**Detail of opening.**

*Opposite page:* Light well.

*Following pages:* Southern facade viewed from the interior.

This slanting wall is the buttress of a building that has been overturned. The concrete shell shows signs of slow subsidence. The curves of the facades seem to be warped by a relentless erosion and the openings in the walls form a series whose pattern has been lost in time, but still bears, written or painted, the simple tokens of the pilgrims. The *brise-soleil* wedged in crevices stand like primitive anthropomorphic idols. The floor inside has tipped up as if it had been worn out by the knees of crowds praying in a light which seems to have found its way by boring through matter. In the thickness of a wall, there are two niches which have been deserted by recumbent statues; all over, there are objects magnificently placed, waiting for celebrations whose rites are ancient. Ronchamp is a coalescence of time, a brilliant voyage through Christianity staged with the necessary twist of drama, exaltation and fervor.
The only glimpse of Le Corbusier is that of a young man climbing another inspiring hill, forty years earlier, and discovering the very subtle effects produced by the asymmetrical volumes of the ruined Acropolis. Ronchamp is rooted in his sense of marvel.

Interior with altars, pulpit and baptismal fonts.

In 1935, on the transatlantic ship taking him to New York for the first time – he was invited by the Museum of Modern Art – Le Corbusier befriended industrialist and art collector André Jaoul. This friendship, which lasted until Jaoul's death in 1954, resulted in two projects, fifteen years apart. The first was a small country house. The first floor was intended to be the kingdom of the four Jaoul boys, with a play room and a bedroom. It was made of wooden boards affixed to a fir-trunk frame, a quick building method that anticipated the theoretical studies of the war years, particularly the prototypes of MAS, "maison montée à sec" (dry assembly house) of 1939-1940, and the Murondin construction, or cell, developed for emergencies and temporary shelter (1940-1942). The small wooden house of the 30s did not see the light of day. But, in June 1951, André Jaoul and his son Michel, who had become a father himself, asked Le Corbusier to build them villas, on the same piece of land in Neuilly on the outskirts of Paris.

The initial design, submitted by English architect Clive Entwhistle for a large three-story building, had been abandoned. Le Corbusier designed two separate villas, set perpendicular to each other with identical layouts: entrance, kitchen, living room and library on the ground floor, bedrooms on the first and second floors. The construction principle of the two villas, named A and B, is identical: a structure of three load-bearing walls in solid brick that form two uneven bays. Above the bays there is a concrete beam. Each villa is topped by a Catalan vault. The dimensions are a strict application of the Modulor: one bay is 3.66 meters, the other is 2.66 meters, the height of the whole is 2.66 meters under the lintels. The materials – concrete, brick and wood – are left rough. The wind would sow a haphazard garden on the roof. The Jaoul houses and the villas in Ahmedabad were the last private residencies in the Corbusian works. Private home gave way, until the architect's death in 1965, to the issues of mass housing and the large developments of Nantes-Rezé, Berlin, Meaux, Briey-en-Forêt and Firminy.

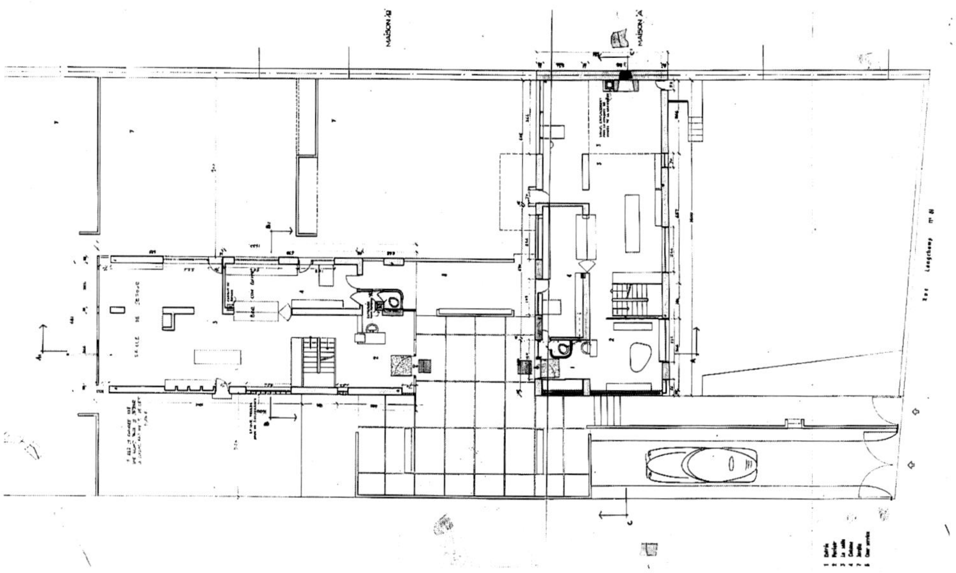

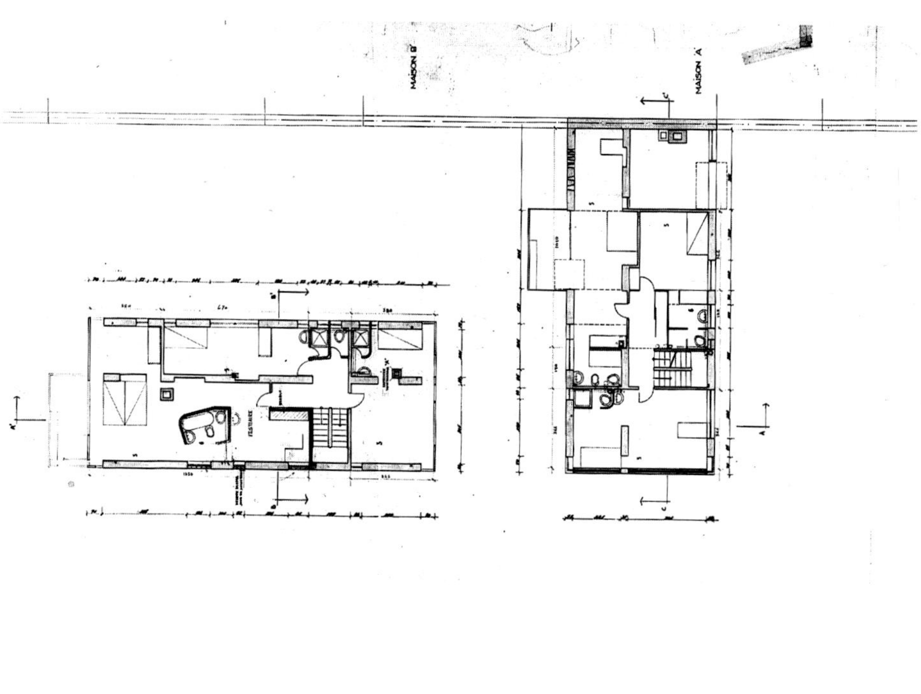

# Maisons Jaoul

**Project architect:** Le Corbusier.
**Client:** André Jaoul, industrialist, and his son Michel.
**Construction dates:** 1951-1955.
**Description:** Principal residences of André Jaoul and of his son.
**Location:** 81 bis, rue de Longchamp, Neuilly-sur-Seine, France.
**Current condition:** The houses were restored by Jacques Michel in 1988-1990.

"A" and "B" houses and garden.

*Opposite page:* "A" house, northeastern corner.

*Following pages:* "B" house, western facade.

Built in a chic suburb for an industrialist and his family, there are two maisons Jaoul. Both harsh and hospitable, they constitute a warning: the world of appearances dulls the mind. The subtext: architecture greatly contributes to that dulling of the mind by making large artefacts that are, for the most part, resting places for thought.

During the 50s, appearances were changing. The environment transformed itself to become modern. Minds mobilized themselves, there were huge changes in the field of urban planning, in the construction of buildings, in the design of architecture, the consumption of objects and the development of networks.

In France, Le Corbusier designed, better than anyone else, architectural and urban shapes that suited the modern world. His works were well advanced and seemed to be logically following the steps of a remarkable process of maturation that began with the "purist villas" and led to Chandigarh. If one adds his sweeping urban theories and interest in furniture, one obtains a perfectly articulated intellectual construct that inspires respect. The CIAM – Congrès international d'architecture moderne (International Modern Architecture Congress) – in which all of the avant-garde was gathered, supported these works. Every modern architect turned to it before starting a project.

The two small Jaoul houses called the soundness of that all too simple construction into question.

Essentially, they are clearly modern: the rational way they are laid out, planned and built, the neat transitions of the program's elements, the intertwining of spaces, the roof garden (perhaps ironic).

But, with incredible aplomb, the two houses stubbornly refuse to cite any of the obligatory metaphors of modernity: no reference to the world of machines and industry, no concern for lightness or the work on light, aesthetic treatment that ignores abstraction, no attention paid to the "five points" of Corbusian vocabulary. Nothing, except bland support walls, bricks with intentionally sloppy joints, thick Catalan vaults, wild grass on the roof and a bit of plywood. It is not even traditional construction, which presumes a taste for good work. The technical nature of the maisons Jaoul, erected in the center of the prosperous Parisian suburb of Neuilly, evokes perfunctory construction methods.

The maisons Jaoul are hard to swallow, they are rough and wild on the outside. Le Corbusier was known to be short-tempered: he must have had a fit here. It may have been possible to calm him by invoking excuses as explanations. The world went through a major economic crisis, a second world war, and massive rebuilding that badly tarnished the idea

of the "industrial production of buildings." Le Corbusier must have lost many of his illusions as to the "precise beauty of machines" and the clearsightedness of the entrepreneurs of his era. On the other hand, he experienced the timeless in Algeria and in India. He drew closer to the Mediterranean and its mythology. Should these arguments be heard? Le Corbusier would have made amends, invested in the basic values to the detriment of his previous works – too white, too abstract and refined. A factual and formal analysis of his buildings generally interprets the maisons Jaoul as an about-turn. This way of seeing things, which limits itself to appearances, is incomplete.

Corbusian architecture is a form of gymnastics intended to make the mind work: it invents mental exercises. The forms it takes – one must be concerned with the look – appeal to the observer's intelligence. To have access to the mind, the undertaking goes through the body: the toppling of the senses invigorates the mind.

Take, for example, the villa Savoye: its hypnotic whiteness, its steep ramps, its disconcerting articulations agitate the body to communicate emotions. A very rare moment comes about, when the spirit of the architecture takes over from senses overwhelmed by the architectural devices, by the loss of physical signals, by disconcerting demands.

Perhaps upheaval is the constant in Corbusian architecture. It keeps the mind from resting on certitudes and halting at appearances. It constantly pushes the mind.

The result is an architecture that does not immediately try to seduce. 
On the contrary, it cultivates a line which maintains distance and demands a moment of adaptation, a hesitation that will prove conducive to reflection. The architecture of the maisons Jaoul grates in order to stimulate the senses. In fact, one must become accustomed to them and question their nature. Le Corbusier cultivated the art of taking the opposite view. He enjoyed upsetting the balance. He was attracted by the fall. If that were not the case, then why did he insist on referring to airplanes and cars in the 20s? They hardly flew, they ran without any guarantee. These machines carried within the very image of their accident and the new thrill they promised demanded courage and physical involvement. Why did he design these houses on *pilotis* with a bit of nature on the roof, if it weren't to overthrow the order of the simplest things and put them off-balance: by lifting the bulk of the construction off the ground and placing on top what is naturally found underneath? Why did he use abstraction if not to test the nerve of his rich clients accustomed to the accumulation of material goods and forced by this abstraction to get rid of them?

Is it possible to imagine Le Corbusier face to face with an Airbus

**Bedroom, closet and colored pipes.**



***Opposite page:*** **Living room, detail.**

**Living room. stairway and "Catalan vault."**

airplane or a Renault Safrane? They do not frighten anyone; nowadays, the car is an object associated with regressive tendencies. Doubtless, in 1950, he thought that architectural modernity had become a look, a style, with its recipes, masters and traitors. A modernity which had known how to be convincing, outside of the architectural range, by serving the production of a profusion of objects whose use becomes reassuring by unifying behavior.

The maisons Jaoul do not worry about being convincing. They establish such a brutal degree of materiality that their physical presence becomes strange in a world fascinated by dress, style and packaging and reassured by these very civilized forms of puritanism. From that perspective, the two houses are obscene: they were shocking because they changed the relation of the human body to architecture. If they were deemed primitive, it was because primitive people were thought of as naked.

The maisons Jaoul dissect the corpus of modern architecture. They are its cut-away diagram. They do not take the body of the observer for an architectural promenade that could move him. His very flesh is involved; the action of the architecture acts upon it. His organism is the target.

From the entrance, one stumbles across the toilet, and the obsessive presence of en suite bathrooms is a blunt reminder of the necessity for personal hygiene. The heating and plumbing pipes left apparent are a successful metaphor for the circulatory system because they are shocking. The floor is warm like skin, an underground network runs through it, conferring its energy. Finally, the flesh: red brick, so bare, around concrete so untreated it looks like a shining piece of meat on the bone, no longer to be seen in the butcher shops of our cities, but rather on market stalls in India or Algeria. Delicate stomachs turn: if it were necessary to come up with an image for the emotion felt, it would be found in the works of Soutine. Nothing here sets the mind at ease.

# Millowners' Association Building

**Project architect:** Le Corbusier.

**Client:** Ahmedabad Millowners' Association, represented by its secretary, Surottam Hutheesing.

**Construction dates:** 1951-1954.

**Description:** Building for association headquarters, with offices, conference rooms and auditorium.

**Location:** Ranchhodial Marg, Savarangpura, Ahmedabad, Gujarat. The rear facade of the building is on the west bank of the Sabarmati river.

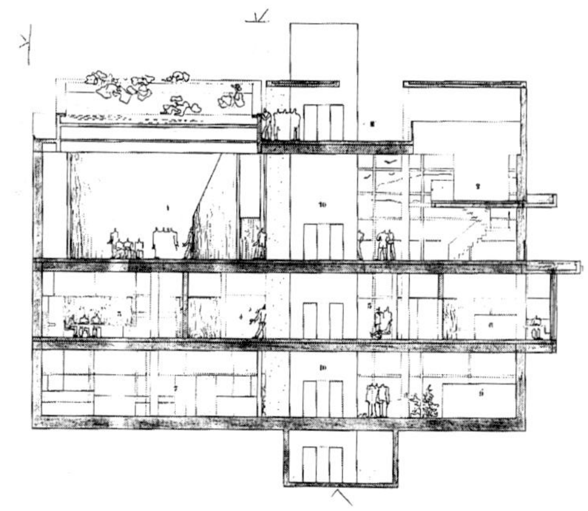

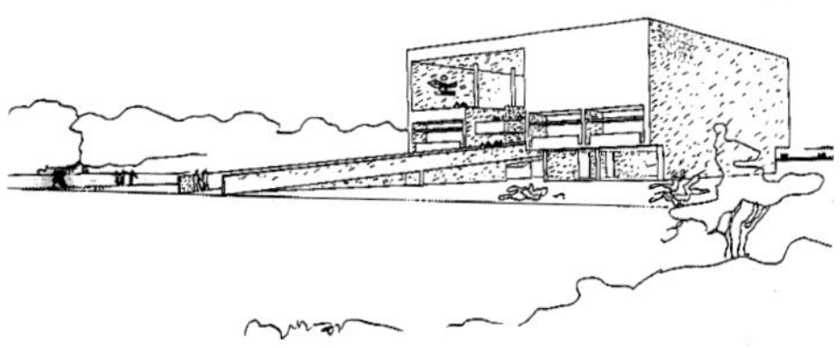

From one Indian city to the other, Le Corbusier echoed his own projects: for example, the plans for Ahmedabad preceded and often announced those for the new capital of Punjab. However the contexts were diametrically opposed: in Chandigarh , the privilege of virginity; in Ahmedabad, becoming part of the very rich architectural heritage of a city dating back to the 15th century, erected in the reign of the enlightened Prince Ahmed Shah. As a result of this tradition of elegance and culture, perpetuated and maintained by the textile industry, the French architect's plans were realized in the former Gujarati capital.

Le Corbusier's detour or "kidnapping" by Ahmedabad was instigated by a well-known family, the Sarabhais. Gira and Gautam Sarabhai, artist and architect respectively, were the first to convince the mayor of the city (and their brother-in-law), Chinubhai Chimanbhai, to call on "the soul of Chandigarh " to construct a cultural center and museum on the banks of the Sabarmati river. Then it was the turn of the mayor's cousin, Surottam Hutheesing, secretary of the Millowners' Association, to commission the Association headquarters, on a piece of land which was also on the banks of the Sabarmati river. On the banks of the river there was also the ashram Satyagraha of Mahatma, today the Gandhi Memorial.

For the flower of this "Manchester of India," the capitalist aristocracy of the textile industry – philanthropic, learned, cosmopolitan and freedom fighters from the beginning – this European pacing the Gujarat, notebook in hand, thoroughly enjoying it, was creating the Indian architecture of modern times. The Millowners' Association was allotted a "little palace" placed under the sign of the *brise-soleil*. On the courtyard side is an "architectural promenade" and on the garden side, a view of the activities taking place on the banks of the river below: dyers, shepherds, and so on.



# Villa Shodan

**Project architect:** Le Corbusier.

**Client:** Initially, Surottam Hutheesing, secretary of the Millowners' Association, then Shyamubhai Shodan and his family.

**Construction dates:** 1951-1956.

**Description:** Five-story house.

**Location:** Ellis Bridge, Ahmedabad, Gujarat.

In the spring of 1951, following their official commissions for the cultural center and the Millowners' Association Building, the mayor of Ahmedabad, Chinubhai Chimanbhai and Surottam Hutheesing – both energetic, influential men – asked the architect to build their private residences.

Passionately interested in modern architecture, Chimanbhai was eagerly looking forward to the new house: he lived in a mansion with his family and wanted a compact house, modern and spacious, with three bedrooms and separate verandahs. As for Hutheesing, since he was a bachelor, his residence was designed with a view to the fulfillment of his social obligations.

The architect submitted practically identical plan for a five-story palace to both clients: a magisterial cube, covered by a stone parasol, with protective *brise-soleil* that opened to allow fresh air to circulate, and a ramp leading up to the terraces with roof gardens set in untreated concrete. No doubt, the two men had expected simple, less costly two-story villas. Their collaboration with Le Corbusier soon came to an end. The construction of the Chimanbhais' villa, which had started as a sort of wager, was soon stopped, as the mayor's wife found it too extravagant. The young secretary of the Millowners' Association, who was a sharp businessman, sold the plans for his villa to Shyamubhai Shodan.

Fitted with a pure horizontal slab, Dom-ino fashion, and with a triple-size terrace with intertwined platforms, the villa Shodan is close to the enchanted world of *A Thousand and One Nights*, for the stairway offers graceful views – characteristic of Indian miniatures – of the garden. Le Corbusier also drew inspiration from the traditional layout of terraces as "separate bedrooms," called *barsaatis;* as he wrote in his *Carnets* in November 1955, he tried to give Shyamubhai Shodan a house of freedoms: "He goes out of his little house onto the first, the second terrace, in the shade, sheltered. In perpetually moving air. He climbs on the roof and sleeps there. Everywhere, he and his guests are sheltered, captivated and enchanted."

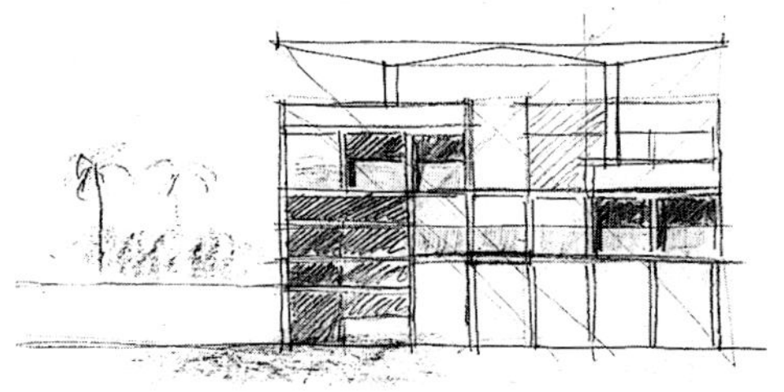

# Ahmedabad, India

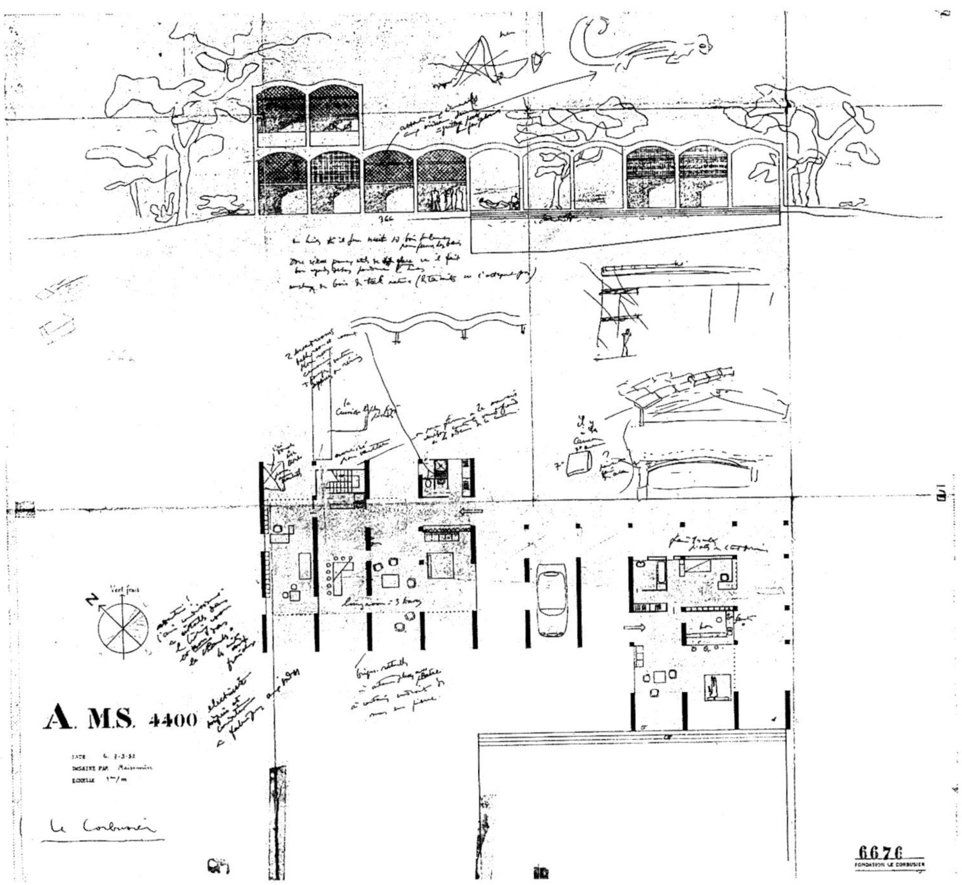


## Villa Sarabhai

**Project architect:** Le Corbusier.
**Client:** Manorama Sarabhai.
**Construction dates:** 1951-1956.
**Description:** Family house for Mrs. Sarabhai and her son Anand.
**Location:** Shahibag, Ahmedabad, Gujarat. The house is located in the midst of a green space called the Retreat, in the inner suburbs of Ahmedabad.

Manorama Sarabhai, the recently widowed sister of Ahmedabad's mayor, wanted a discreet house, set in the luxuriant tropical paradise named the Retreat; this name seeming to call for an equally restrained attitude. Furthermore, like many of the millowners, Manorama Sarabhai was part of the very influential Jain community whose commandments – non-violence and the inviolability of Nature – were close to those of the ahimsa of Mahatma Gandhi.
Interior and exterior were blended with the tendrils of a garden, house with large bay windows swallowed by the vegetation, bordered by a roof-lawn. In Shahibag, Le Corbusier offered his own interpretation of the Jain teachings for the benefit of his client and her little boy Anand. The villa Sarabhai is not typical of his Indian buildings: its elegant architecture is modest, inspired by peasant architecture and the royal pavilions and gardens of the Mogul Empire. It also has a slight touch of juvenile mischief: the toboggan run from the roof garden into the swimming-pool was an idea Anand Sarabhai whispered into the ear of his accomplice.
Structured by the repeated use of the vault, the villa Sarabhai was the last of the "houses with Catalan vaults" designed by the architect. Most likely inspired by the docks of Auguste Perret in Casablanca (1915), the vaulted roof was used by Le Corbusier as early as 1919 for the Monol house.
During a trip in 1928, he rediscovered it in the Casa Gaudí, explored its possibilities in his apartment/studio in porte Molitor (1931-1934) as well as in the Henfel house, built in Saint-Cloud in 1935, and reintroduced the vault in the 1950s, with the Jaoul houses in Neuilly-sur-Seine which are contemporary with the Indian villa.

As the visitor draws near, the building shows no sign of life. It is entrenched behind an even assembly of concrete planes that blocks off the views. However, there is nothing opaque. In the strong light, the gaze sinks into shade barely dispersed by a large hanging porch set in the geometrical center of the facade. A long ramp leads up to it. The visitor is placed at a distance, precisely where the effects produced by the building are best discovered. Its dignity is impressive from the start, and the palace appears, like in a parade, coated with a rough and noble texture that clothes the approximations of its organs: offices and meeting rooms.

Nothing in it is familiar. This imposing grey mass decides the way in which it is to be approached. The visitor does not follow the ramp that leads toward the entrance; it agrees to pick him up and delivers him, flattered, underneath the porch.

In India, the elephant unrolls his trunk to enable a raw-boned mahout to prop up his feet and grip both its ears. Then, putting his head up with dignity, the elephant lifts his human charge to place it behind his head, in a fold of skin that makes a magnificent rough grey envelope. Although the architecture of Le Corbusier is well thought-out, it is also a matter of flesh. It appeals to the entire body. Head and legs, sight and motion are necessary for those who wish to experience the inner space of the Millowners' Association building.

**Access ramp to the Millowners' Association Building.**

Perched in the middle of the building, unsuccessful in differentiating the inside from the outside, one finds oneself behind facades that act as visual apparatus. Through their prism, the disorderly and elusive excitement of the Indian city is broken up, regulated and straightened until the urban confusion seems comprehensible. It is brought back to a position where it is operable: one can envisage influencing it or projecting ideas onto it. This filter, calculated and built for a group of industrialists, makes available to the entrepreneur, a modern man, a tool to assess his environment. He, from his vantage point, retains his aloofness and profits from the distance necessary for an entrepreneur. His eye sees precisely and his mind is cleared.

The palace is a place for observation, free of anything that can confuse the senses. The arrangement and the diversity of its interior masses compose a sensitive and well-balanced world that is a substitute for the outside world, testing and vague, and chooses to propose only an accomplished version of it. The palace is an ideal city: pure, detached, airy as well. The perfect geometry of the facades offers a glimpse of its enclosed masses – meeting rooms, offices, maintenance quarters – that are objects floating freely in an immaterial dimension. Air goes through the palace, uninterrupted by neither the facades nor the floors,

***Opposite page:*** **Eastern facade with "brise-soleil."**

and escapes through the large perforations placed in a building astonishingly uncluttered by its functions. At the heart of the attached voids running through several levels, the constructed volumes present themselves from more than one angle, thereby establishing connections. One is drawn to discover them. Sufficiently large, with a sufficiently strong presence, these voids constitute a hollow architecture that gives the whole its impalpable, celestial quality. Le Corbusier named that part "space." So the air circulates through the space (failing to cool it). It constantly accompanies the movements of bodies and eyes. All the better as the building has no rough patches that could constrain this flux: no articulation between architecture and decoration, between structure and ornamentation, and no additions that would divert the eye by keeping it focused on accessory objects. The whole thing is circulatory. Architecture is the only power at play; it smoothes perception, makes the glance flow and the body slide.

A restrained palette of materials and colors acts on this dynamic: concrete, stone, white coating, flat tints of bright colors. Through effects of roughness, polish, neutrality or brightness, this damper regulates the speed of the flow, slowing it or speeding it up.

One allows oneself to be taken to enigmatic places, on abandoned galleries, up to the bare terrace: there is no one to meet there. The mills closed down a long time ago and the air only pushes endlessly spinning shadows. The same shadows may be encountered in a metaphysical landscape painted by Giorgio de Chirico.

However, the promenade through the palace is not really solitary, the tension of the internal arrangements still bears witness to Le Corbusier's presence. In silence he moves in front of us on the visiting tour and, as if he were conducting sonorous and dignified music, he points out slowly: here is a curved surface, here is a red wall, further along is a gallery, here a detached column, a table frozen in the cement and so forth. It is magnificent; it is moving. But what an enigma!

**Second floor corner.**



***Opposite page:*** **"Brise-soleil."**

156

**Lobby.**

**Circulation around the conference hall.**

***Opposite page:* First floor and reception.**

*Opposite page:*
Villa Shodan. Facade and "brise-soleil."

Villa Shodan. Entrance facade and patio.

What was the relationship between the Shodan and Sarabhai families, neighbors in the middle of a garden that would be a good address for paradise? While their houses express such different ways of appearing, of entertaining, of enjoying life, what did the families think of each other when they visited?

The Shodan family had a villa built: it is a patrician residence. It displays clear thoughts, speaks loudly and imposes its strong cubic stature. One wants to get close to it. It is not inviting for its front facade is so opaque and severe; it is also proud, topped as it is by a large concrete plane full of panache.

However, if one has the good fortune to please it, it invites one in and lets show, on its other facades, a face that is much more affable. What seemed in the beginning a concrete fortress becomes, facing the garden, an attractive array of wide-open rooms, terraces, nooks and stairways. How many situations there are to experience in this picturesque decor, with its diversely cut planes that inscribe themselves in a perfect square! How many attitudes to adopt! How many stories to tell!

This accumulation of levels, this generous composition where space is plentiful, must certainly go beyond the range of domestic life. To enjoy it thoroughly, a life filled with receptions and pomp should be led. One imagines the crowd of guests colonizing this magnificent roost. The crowd moves elegantly from one level to another: a couple has retreated to a forgotten corner, a group has taken over a stairway, up on the terrace, there are laughing shadows moving about and, on a platform, in front of a crouching orchestra, a dancer turns. The sequence of her movements evokes the women who used to beat their naked feet on the simple terrace of Fatehpur Sikri, following the same rhythms, in front of the mysterious emperor who infinitely admired them and who reigned by entertaining his court.

The influence of the Shodan family was great: the villa is a clear sign of this influence. Huge, playful and enchanting, the villa permitted the Shodans to oblige the crowd they welcomed and entertained. Why climb a small stairway to the fourth-floor terrace to be hit by the glaring sun and, in doing so, neglect the attractions and shade of the garden below? The reason being that, by practicing with application that audacious counterpoint to the splendors of nature, one showed the master of the house that one was impressed by his establishment.

Without the crowd one enjoyed imagining, this place is so large and languorous. It evokes retrenchment at the center of a construction that remakes the world starting with rare impressions and selected experiences. It seems a beautiful toy in which to fantasize about perfect links to the environment. There, one would like to be relieved from an

Views of the villa Shodan. Lawn and swimming pool.

outside that remains cluttered by vegetation that is oppressive in its eternal luxuriance and filled with obscene monkeys, mocking birds and insolent peacocks whose cries do not cover up the immense, constant agitation of the faraway city.

Today, in front of such a mass, built using so many effects, one feels like a destitute prince deserted by his crowd of courtiers. One thinks of a huge shell hollowed by a wave to which no sea creature would no longer lend its body .

The Sarabhai family had a shelter built at the heart of nature. One enters it naturally, like during a stroll through the garden, without bumping into a doorstep, without going through a facade. The shade provided by the tropical plants spills out to the vaults of the construction.

This shelter expresses nothing it would be necessary to explain. It does not feel the need to be impressive: it is evidently satisfied with its location. Free of all vanities, it appears, like statues of wise men, motionless and smiling. It is a retreat, the intense pleasures cultivated here are barely apparent.

Not out of wisdom, more out of ingenuity, Adam might have built it in Paradise. He would not have had to look far for the materials, and he would have assembled them with a simple gesture – a bow at arms length becomes a vault – with the grace that existed before the Fall. He would have done this without hiding anything, without being embarrassed by nakedness. But, no longer alone, having starting to reason and reflect, he would have added a toboggan run directed toward the sky, enjoying thumbing his nose at the forbidden.

What did the Shodan and Sarabhai families say to each other when they paid each other a visit? Certainly, they must have touched upon Le Corbusier. The Shodans would fiercely defend the master's work. The Sarabhais would listen, nodding slightly, their sole argument a smile. Today, the same smile welcomes the hordes of architects walking through their house without altering its harmony. A miracle.

**Villa Sarabhai. Entrance.**

***Opposite page:*** **Villa Sarabhai. Garden terrace.**

***Previous pages:*** **Villa Sarabhai. Garden facade, toboggan run and swimming-pool.**

Villa Sarabhai. Garden pavilion.



Villa Sarabhai. Reception room.

*Le Corbusier on site at la Tourette (1959).*



After having contacted Maurice Novarina in 1950, the Dominican congregation turned to Le Corbusier, following the advice of Father Alain Couturier (friend of the architect). The object of the contract was to build a place for retreats and seminaries able to welcome about a hundred brothers, on the land of an old farm the order had just purchased, facing the little town of Eveux-sur-Arbresle.

In May 1953, the discovery of the site – the slope of a small damp valley surrounded by forests in the Lyon countryside – brought about the first sketches and a design that was never abandoned: a square layout, which includes the slope of the plot and draws on the Cistercian model in Thoronet (the monastery would occasion a journey as well as an erudite and technical correspondence with Father Couturier); access to the building on the middle level (reception, study rooms and seminaries), the two upper floors are for the monks' cells, the lower floors are for communal life (dining hall, chapter, atrium). For this "organisme en descente" (system on a declining slope), Le Corbusier had initially planned to highlight the incline with a processional ramp intended to take the monks up to the cloister on the roof, under the open sky. The idea ended up being abandoned for an assembly. The monastery is U-shaped, closed by the church: a "box" that is an independent wing. As to the cells, they form a *brise-soleil* and opened onto the outside by overhanging loggias; they are reminiscent of the charterhouse of Galuzzo – also called the charterhouse of Ema – near Florence, one the architectural phenomena that most moved Le Corbusier during his stays in the Florentine countryside in 1907 and 1911.

The engineers participated very closely in the genesis of the monastery, working on a site that had taken on an experimental aspect and required, among other things, the contribution of a new company, the company Burdin-Perratone, specializing in works of art and prestressed concrete. It also happens that a young engineer, Iannis Xenakis, played a very important role on the site: he had been a technical assistant at Le Corbusier's rue de Sèvres agency since the Marseilles project and he shared Le Corbusier's taste for mathematics (and the Modulor). For the monastery of la Tourette, the composer of *Metastasis,* to whom Le Corbusier had confided the plans, presented the architect with "musical walls," or undulatory panes of glass as well as "light projecting machine guns."

# Monastery of Sainte-Marie-de-la-Tourette

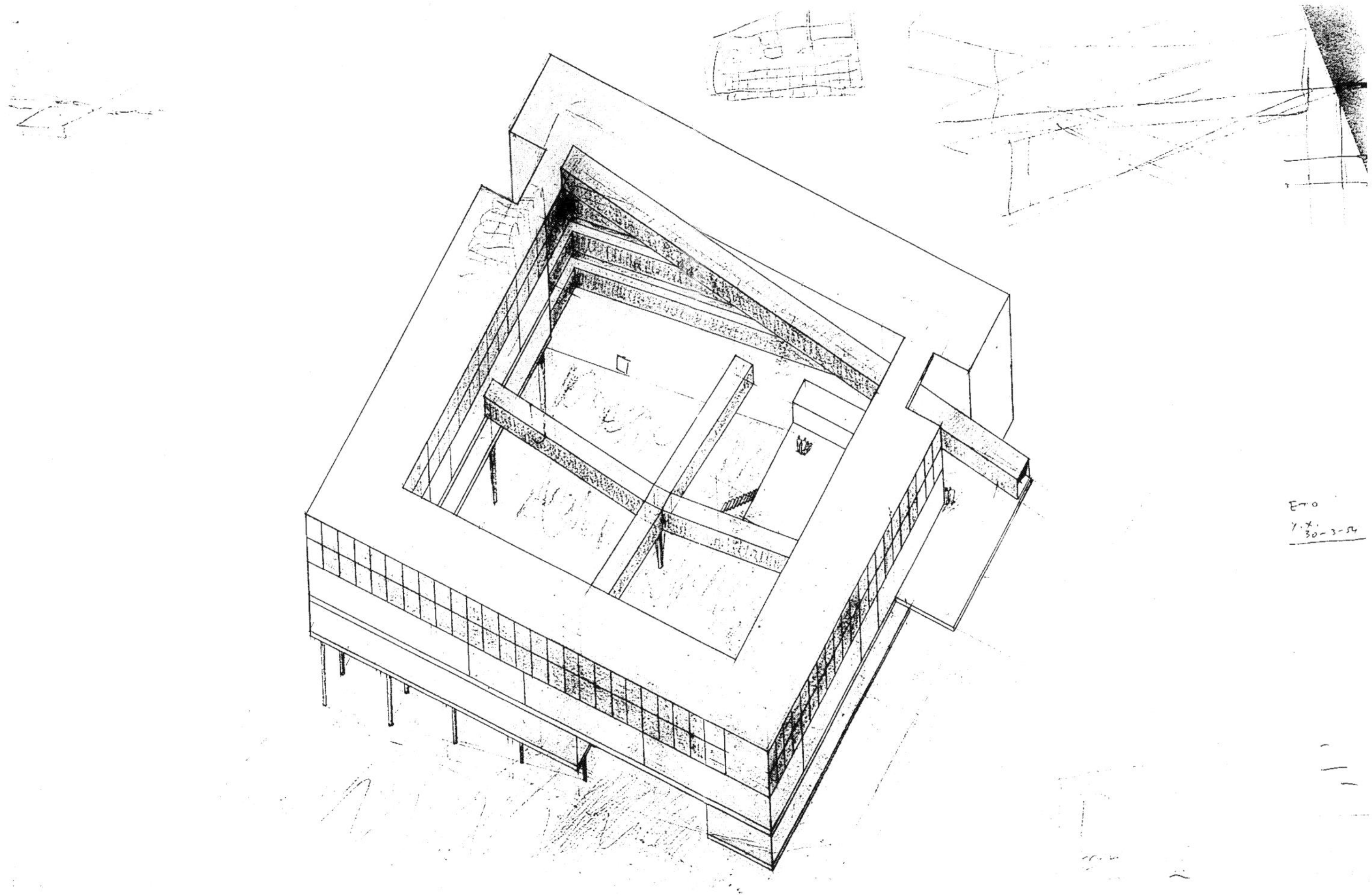



**Project architects:** Le Corbusier with the contribution of Iannis Xenakis.

**Client:** Provincial chapter of the Dominicans of Lyon, under the impetus of Father Couturier and Brother Belaud O.P.

**Construction dates:** 1953-1961. Construction began in August 1956. It was inaugurated on October 19, 1960, in the presence of Cardinal Gerlier and Father Browne, general master of the order.

**Description:** Monastery to house preaching friars during their education and training.

**Location:** Eveux-sur-Arbresle, 27 kilometers from Lyon, France.

**Current condition:** The monastery now welcomes guests. It offers about sixty cells, full board, reservations required.

*Opposte page:* View from a cell on the eastern side.

General view, eastern facade.

Northern facade.

# It is necessary to begin at the beginning.

Religion is a matter of faith. In monasteries, this faith is practised with an exceptional rigor that intimidates the visitor the moment he goes through the gate. The impression is often confused. With only superficial knowledge, one imagines the monastery to be a place of forgetful retreat.

The Dominicans at la Tourette are not retiring. They chose to expose themselves instead of cutting themselves off from the world. By actively participating in the intellectual debates of the secular world, they are working at keeping the wedge of faith and its mystery driven into that world.

At the present time, which crystallizes so fast that we are both dazzled and shocked, they offer the possibility of confronting the religious absolute whose Teachings are timeless. By referring to divine transcendence, they seek to open up the era organized around rational thought to a fundamental doubt. They themselves are exposed to permanent doubt. Grappling with the world, feeling its intellectual attraction, completely delivering to the world what one has learnt from the divine Word, at the risk of seeing one's faith shaken by the freedom to think, is a struggle according to the Dominicans. A Dominican monastery is a fearsome place. Heaven and earth are moved there. It is also a quiet place where a community of monks, having made the vow of poverty, master the organization of its life by very civil means and in an egalitarian spirit.

Le Corbusier did not believe, his faith was not religious in the strict sense of the word. He was not a practising believer, but he had such a wide notion of religion that he assimilated the Dominicans' efforts into his own commitment: they maintain a part of the religious absolute in the world while his architecture communicates a part of the indescribable to the world.

The courage and clearsightedness of the Dominicans is to have understood that, in order to renew itself, sacred architecture must call on thinking that is liberated and radically committed to the century. With great intellectual agility, Le Corbusier extracted timeless sentiments out of a timeless program, thanks to an architecture without precedent.

The monastery of la Tourette is a work of the mind. Its form is unimportant, even less so as the building is deliberately poor just like the monks who have made a vow of poverty.

Among the poor, there is nothing to see after the initial shock of their destitution. Here, there is nothing but rudimentary concrete, incapable of holding a plane or tracing a line. There is nothing impressive about it. Poverty is not an aesthetic: to impose its style would be an unwelcome

*Opposite page:* Church and sacristy facades with "light-emitting machine-guns."

Interior northern facade.
View of the enclosed space.
General southeastern view.

affectation in those who have internalized abnegation. It is not morality: the monks do not need lessons and do not give them either. It is even less the unfortunate result of a very tight budget: the architecture of the monastery at la Tourette has freed itself from material constraints. Its poverty is a choice, a means that clears the mind, ridding it of excess and obliging it to stick to the essential. Destitution is a complex economy that enables the establishment of an unimpeded flow between the movements of the mind and the movements of the body – from thought to reality, from word to matter, in all freedom.

Le Corbusier was 65 years old when he started work on la Tourette. His great fame allowed him to dispense with justifications or explanations. Each of his works was long-awaited and would be admired. His age and standing allowed him so much freedom that it became a test.

La Tourette is an exercise in detachment. The building does not rest on anything. It does not call on any commonplace or convention, apart from its square design – the traditional layout for monasteries. This building, new, detached from things already seen, unexpected, seems to have been designed from notes taken during a dream.

Varied, split up, sliced, badly joined to the point of being chaotic, the building evokes the transience of a thought deviating from its thread in order to find new connections. It is impossible to grasp. In everything, its sketchiness takes on the quality of dreams when they skim over things, assembling them curiously and simplifying their appearance. Thus, it is cast in a unique and fluid material – concrete – to the point of obsession: the glazed "undulatory" facades would have, in the reasonable world, been constructed for the same price in wood or steel and not concrete. It is also loose, again like in the dreams that visit places without concern for their limits or their links: the building is attached to the ground as it comes. It is unconcernedly detached from it, one sees underneath it, and its *pilotis* – part-matchstick, part-arcade – do not evoke the will to deal with gravity.

Beyond dreams, its aloofness recalls the freshness of a sketch, the dynamic of working on a model, the techniques which materialize intuition in next to no time. The monastery of la Tourette resembles a work in progress and retains the fragile grace of certain models: the thinness and grain of its walls evoke crude cardboard, cut to the quick, then roughly put back together without concern for joins dripping with too much glue applied too quickly, leaving regrets and additions apparent.

At the end of his life, Matisse invented the technique of paper cutouts and won a tremendous amount of freedom, – airy is how he qualified it. He liked these simple patterns of colour, outlined on large sheets

Roof garden.

Church steeple.

Stairway pavilion.

painted with gouache, best when they were pinned on the walls of his studio – fragile, curling up at the edges, available – rather than flat on a canvas or tightly fitted onto the page of a book.

The monastery of la Tourette is a paper cutout that curls up at the edges. It is not so for lack of means. Matisse did not cut up his paper because he could no longer hold his paintbrush. In his last works, Titian did not paint with large brushes or with his fingers because his eyesight was failing. To each of them, growing old offered freedom and detachment, not those sought by youth, but more radical, even more hurried and ultimately more profound.

The dream freedom of Le Corbusier, that of his movements, opened the way for a series of overturnings which appeared right from the monastery's conception: the elements of the monastery's plan were split up, isolated and manipulated until they produced a paradoxical form of architecture. The bottom is on top, the outside is inside, the sky and the earth are hurly-burly.

Traditionally, the monks wander along the quadrangle of the cloister, around a garden that represents a perfect world, away from the frenzy and corruption of the times. Their cells and the different rooms in the monastery open onto this square of calm. The monastery is inward looking. At la Tourette, the ambulatory is set up on the rooftops, surrendered to the turmoil of a huge impassioned sky. At the center of the quadrilateral formed by the buildings, a tumult of clashing forms meets nature. Wild grass covers the rooftops and grows freely underneath the building. The earth itself seems to turn under the monastery hanging from its skimpy ties without managing to pull it along, like the swell of the ocean leaves the ship where it is.

As for the rest, the monastery is outward looking: it lets the views lose themselves in the steep slopes of an hilly environment. At the center of this arrangement, the monks cross each other at the junction of ramps going in opposite directions.

There is nothing that reassures or comforts the soul: one must stand firmly here.

Each part of the monastery is isolated, then juxtaposed with its neighbors in a series of independent sequences. The feeling of unity is not sought; the idea of wholeness is not communicated.

In order to establish these contrasts, Le Corbusier broke up the masses, based his work on additions and used thwarted assemblies of shapes and textures. The whole is rough and incongruous like a "machine célibataire."

The historical, Suprematist, Neoplasticist and purist avant-gardes also used fragmentation, but were still concerned with general composition.

**Circulation of the interior facade.**

**Refectory.**

However complex it might have been, this will tended to bring architecture closer to the balance achieved in painting or sculpture. Here, the will to compose or to organize is absent. Randomness seems to prevail. The goals are the same as those of the avant-garde – approaching the real, remaining tuned in to the era, being exposed to its constantly renewed energies – but the means are different.

Here, the messianic visions and great intentions that wanted to force the course of events were followed by the expression of the fluidity and ambiguity of the real. The prevailing sentiment was of the inanity of human efforts that tried to circumscribe time once and for all. Henceforth, it would be preferable to follow the changing course of reality, and only a slackening of architecture, an extreme suppleness of its joints, would make sticking to it possible – in the way a piece of clothing falls to accompany the body's movements instead of restraining them.

Literature had already freed itself from the linear narrative by setting in motion diverging points of view which it arranged in sequence without worrying too much about the way they were linked. Literature was no longer narrated. Music was no longer hummed (even less so the music of Xenakis who inspired the "undulatory facades"). Dance no longer followed music and refused to stage prince and swan stories. Painters sought the body's automatisms, manifestations of the unconscious, the abandonment of the conditioned gesture, and excluded any form of composition.

La Tourette cultivates a form of disappointment as to the impossibility of realizing the perfect shape of the monastic square in the heart of an era incapable of feeling for this simple image of perfection. This disappointment is made clear by the incompleteness of the cloister's quadrangle and by the anxious additions which saturate the space. The original nudity is no longer permitted. But this disappointment, after the Fall, did not stop Le Corbusier from being ironic: he designed entrance houses in the shape of Greek shepherds' huts, planted slanted *pilotis* that are halves of arcades and, what is more, acted as if he left everything unfinished, as if he let everything go. He pretended to disappear and left dumbfounded the objects thrown in the middle of the fragmented quadrangle, then, reaching the balcony on the south wing, contemplated the whole thing from that enigmatic roost.

It was the sea, withdrawing, that must have left these broken rooftops, eaten up by vegetation, stuck with slanting tubes, these parts of raised ramps, these lumpy walls, perforated in places or laminated and cracked, this huge shell of a church as well, battered, with a slanted levelling.

It is so lax that there is nothing to see in the church. No pictorial

**Crypt.**

 **Church.**

representations, Le Corbusier had warned. No subtle mystery: the interior space is entirely deducted from the exterior volume of the building which closes the quadrangle to the north. A few centimeters of concrete separate the inside from the outside: prayers from heaven. There is grey concrete on the walls and on the slanted ceiling, grey cement on the floor: one is close to a state of sensory deprivation. Nothing to see then, before having undergone a preliminary visual hygiene.

Then and only then, once one has gotten rid of everything that clutters perception, will one feel the effect of what Le Corbusier called "unspeakable architecture." One understands that it is necessary to contain the feelings it inspires, and the only thing left is to act with discretion when it comes to a subject which concerns the monks so deeply. As if, apart from daily and persistent worship in this place, which one discovers to be liquid when one's eyes open, the emotions felt evaporated in the time it took to expose them.

Quickly and almost as if breaking and entering, past a small door, having gone down a dark stairway, one crosses underneath the church, by following a narrow passageway, to end up in the chapels. It is a dead end. There, everything dances on a slanted floor full of accidents, in the heart of a sort of precarious hut enveloped in concrete pleated like rough felt and daubed with colours. The bodies are turned over, one trips, one wonders if balance can be maintained here. Everything is consumed. The officiating priests, monks in their habits with white hoods and scapulars, walking slowly and cautiously, perform the liturgical gestures. Their movements in this uncertain place have a magical echo for the non-believer. May the Church forgive him! The object of the celebration – he thinks – is to summon the spirits, then, like in legends, make them come down from three large colored wells, from three luminous clouds.

It might be the umbilicus, although, nothing being certain, that remains to be seen.

Views from the roof.

*Opposite page:* Access ramp to the church.

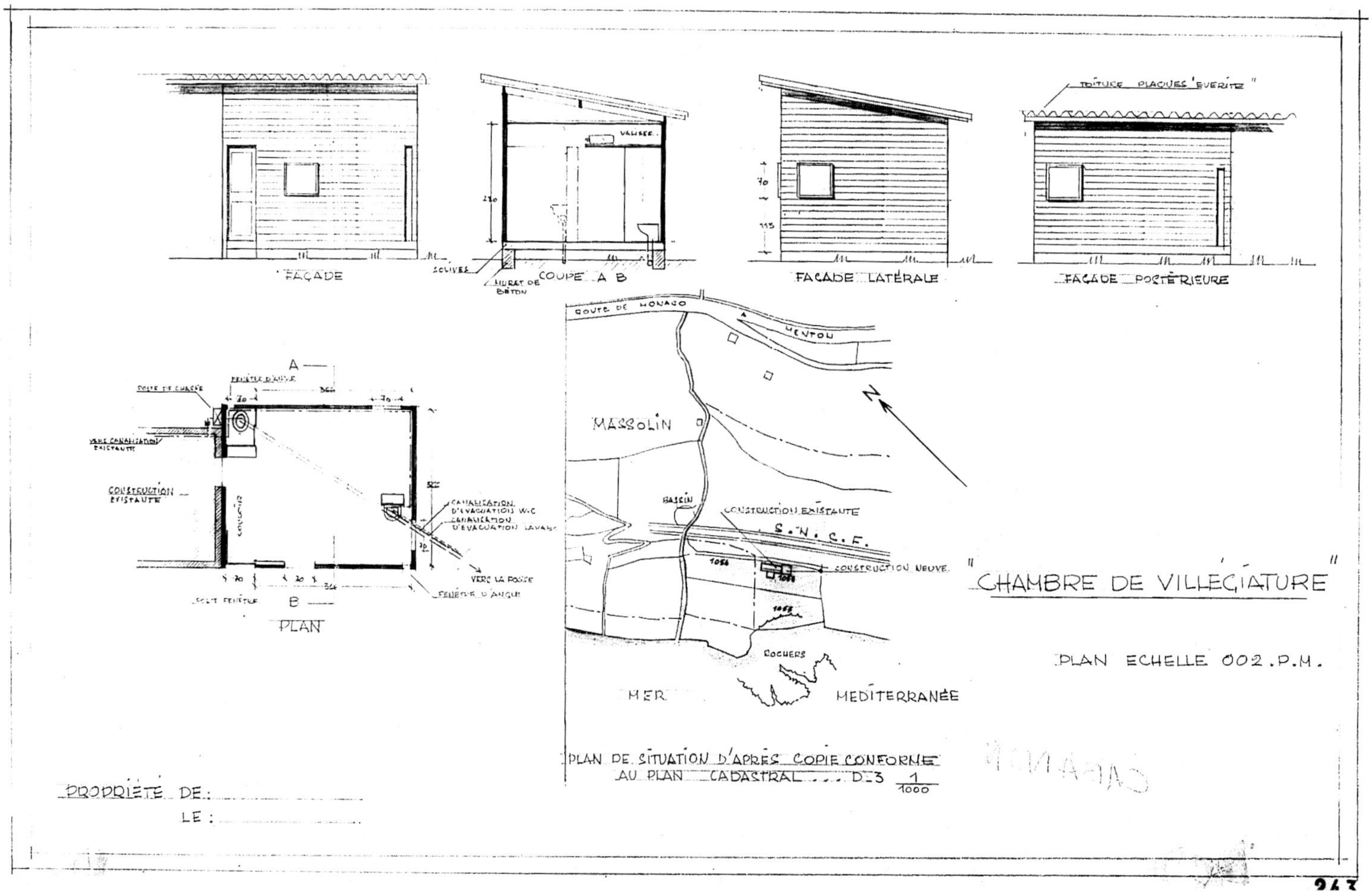




The first idea for the little hut was sketched on the corner of a table in a restaurant on December 30, 1951. It was a present for Yvonne, intended for getting away, set on a slope above a cove, overlooking the sea and Monaco. A square cell, the dimensions of the Modulor, light by two windows, 70 centimeters per side. The whole hut was constructed in wood by Le Corbusier's friend Charles Barberis. Le Corbusier painted the floor of his "boat cabin" in yellow and one panel in green; in 1956, he created a mural to decorate the entrance, the only element of decor. The Mediterranean sea, the sun, the fresh air and friendship do the rest. And so, just a few strides from the famous E-1027 house of Eileen Gray and Jean Badovici in Roquebrune where they had enjoyed going before building their "cabanon," the Le Corbusiers chose very humble accommodation for themselves, set on the same grounds – and equally modest – as the little tavern of the Rebutato brothers who became their hosts and friends.

This is where Le Corbusier designed the ROQ project (1948-1950), a study for a honeycomb standard housing in Roquebrune, followed by the ROB plan (1952-1955) for five vacation units to be built on Roberto Rebutato's piece of land in Cap-Martin. For lack of money, they turned out to be five "camping" units made of wooden boards and were delivered in kit form by Barberis' workshop in Ajaccio, Corsica, to be assembled on site (1957).

# Le cabanon

*Le Corbusier at the cabanon (1952).*



**Project architect and client:** Le Corbusier.

**Construction dates:** 1951-1952.

**Description:** Minimal housing with view of the sea and corners designed for sleep, washing, etc. In 1954, a mini summer studio, measuring 2 by 4 meters, was added on the side of the terrace.

**Location:** Restaurant *L'Etoile de mer*, a little path on the seaside toward Menton, Cap-Martin, Alpes-Maritimes, France.

Opposite page: View of Monte-Carlo

Facade, earth platform and window.

Following pages: The cabanon and tree.

# 366 by 366 by 266 centimeters:

the cabanon is not large. Le Corbusier built it for his own use, and this series of figures is more important than the object it defines.

With the cabanon, this great mind, who paid equal attention to modest or ambitious projects, realized the minutest application of the Modulor, a rule applied without fail until the plans for Chandigarh.

The temptation to make the cabanon a summary of the master's thinking or to extract the root of the Modulor from it is strong. One must resist that temptation. Generalities are too often established on the basis of the observation of secondary facts; thus, complex systems based on small occurrences are hastily constructed. It is like letting oneself be convinced that an apple falling from a tree divulged the secrets of celestial mechanics.

If the cabanon was definitely designed by Le Corbusier, it is not particularly meaningful in terms of his work since each of his buildings constitutes a radical argument supporting theoretical positions. The cabanon says nothing. Le Corbusier lived there: that is all.

Its tiny dimensions fit as close as they possibly can the body of its illustrious resident and provide moving clues about the life he led there. The size of the cabanon is similar to the size of a trunk where a selection of essential personal belongings is ingeniously stored. If one opens it, the life of the owner is displayed without modesty.

In the cabanon, there are two beds, a sink, a toilet and a table. Le Corbusier enjoyed living there naked. But the lack of comfort, like the nuisance caused by handling the trunk, is moderated by the desire for movement and the taste for action.

There is no place in this confined space for boredom to sneak in or for laziness to rest itself. The cabanon sends one back outside to fresh air, sun, and swimming in the sea. It is less a place for retreat than a halt between long journeys: from India to the United States, from Japan to South America. Do not accumulate an inheritance that must be kept up, it advises, do not get encumbered with anything that forces you to return to the place where material concerns occupy the mind. For the work of the intellectual, a little hut, built a few meters away, is sufficient. It modestly indicates that no shape can set or represent the developments of the Corbusian growth. A couple of boards stuck together took care of the shelter function, and thinking was not constrained in there until Le Corbusier decided to make it result in the shapes of the buildings he was constructing somewhere else in the world.

The hut is like a kettle. Hermetic enough for thinking to remain fluid, but with enough cracks between the boards for thinking to be able to escape, once it has been sublimated, and go on to condense elsewhere,

in Chandigarh, Boston or Tokyo. In Cap-Martin, fully caught up in his thoughts, busy with his friendships, sunning and enjoying the sea, Le Corbusier did not waste any time when it came to dying. On August 27, 1965, he suffered a heart attack while he was swimming.
He thus brought about a final, thrilling manipulation of scale.
From the Mediterranean sea to his grave, which was designed like a tiny piece of architecture and where his wife already lay, the coffin, barely larger than his body, broke its journey twice.
The first stop was in proportion with a mind tempted by universality: in the monastery at la Tourette, Dominicans watched over his remains and prayed for the skies to open up.
The second stop, full of drama and ceremonial display, was a production which he would undoubtedly have appreciated. The coffin was shown between two rows of Republican Guards in the Cour carrée of the Louvre. During a nocturnal ceremony, André Malraux delivered the eulogy in which he invoked architectural geniuses, poets, imperishable works, capital cities, rivers and mountains. Words such as these are engraved at the Panthéon.
A conclusion that was the synthesis of Corbusian play between sacred and profane, between his own detachment and the spectacular forms of his glory.

**Wash-basin corner.**

**Entrance with mural by Le Corbusier.**

***Opposite page:*** **Rest corner.**

L-C

Charles-Edouard Jeanneret was born in La Chaux-de-Fonds, Neuchâtel, Switzerland, on October 6, 1887.

**Projects built in La Chaux-de-Fonds:**
*With René Chapallaz*
1905. Villa Fallet.
1908. Villa Stotzer.
1908. Villa Jacquemet.

*Individual projects*
1912. Jeanneret House, called "Maison blanche."
1912. Villa Favre-Jacquot, in Le Locle.
1916. Scala cinema.
1916. Villa Schwob, called "Villa turque."

**First projects built in France:**
1917. Water tower, Podensac, Gironde.
1917. Hydroelectric factory, L'Isle-Jourdain, Vienne.
1917. Worker's house, Saint-Nicolas-d'Aliermont, Seine-Maritime.

*Under the name Le Corbusier*
1921. Interior, Villa Berque, Paris.

**Projects built with Pierre Jeanneret:**
1922. Villa Besnus, Vaucresson, Hauts-de-Seine, France.
1922. Studio/apartment of Amédée Ozenfant, Paris.
1923. La petite maison, Corseaux, near Vevey, Switzerland.
1923-25. Villas La Roche and Jeanneret-Raaf, Paris.
1923. Residence/studio Lipchitz, Boulogne-sur-Seine, Hauts-de-Seine, France.
1923. Residence/studio Miestchaninoff, Boulogne-sur-Seine, Hauts-de-Seine, France.
1923-27. Residence/studio Ternisien, Boulogne-sur-Seine, Hauts-de-Seine, France (destroyed in 1935).
1923-25. Cité de Lège, Gironde, France.
1924. Maison du Tonkin, Bordeaux (destroyed in 1975).
1924-27. Quartier Frugès, Pessac, Gironde, France.
1924-26. Pavillon de l'Esprit nouveau, Arts décoratifs exhibition, (destroyed in 1926).
1924-28. Residence/studio Planeix, Paris.
1926. Residence/studio Guiette, Anvers, France.
1926-27. Annex to the palais du Peuple de l'Armée du Salut (Salvation Army), Paris.
1926-27. Villa Cook, Boulogne-sur-Seine, Hauts-de-Seine, France.
1926-28. Villas Stein and De Monzie, Vaucresson, Hauts-de-Seine, France.
1927-28. Pavillon Nestlé, for the Paris, Bordeaux and Marseilles fairs (demolished).
1927-30. Villas Church, Ville-d'Avray, Hauts-de-Seine (destroyed in 1965).
1927. Two houses at Weissenhof, Stuttgart, Germany.
1928-31. Villa Savoye, Poissy, Yvelines, France.
1928-31. Villa Baizeau, Carthage, Tunisia.
1929-30. Floating shelter of the Salvation Army, Paris.
1929-31. Villa de Mandrot, Le Pradet, France.
1929-32. Interior of Count Charles de Bestegui's apartment (destroyed).
1929-33. Cité de refuge of the Salvation Army, Paris.
1929-33. Pavillon suisse at the Cité universitaire de Paris.
1929-35. Centrosoyuz, Moscow.
1930-32. Clarté Building, Geneva.
1931-34. Building at 24, rue Nungesser-et-Coli, Paris/Boulogne.
1934-35. Henfel weekend house, La Celle-Saint-Cloud, Yvelines, France.
1935. Villa Le Sextant, La Palmyre-Les Mathes, Charente-Maritime, France.
1936. Ministry of National Education (with O. Niemeyer and L. Costa), Rio de Janeiro.
1936-37. Pavillon des Temps nouveaux, 1937 Exposition, Paris (destroyed).
1938-39. Interior of Centre scientifique de la main d'œuvre (CSMO), Paris (destroyed).
1939-40. Centre de réadaptation et de gymnastique pour les jeunes chômeurs, Paris. (destroyed).
1939-40. Occasional schools and portable constructions (with Jean Prouvé).

*Chandigarh* (1951-1965)
1951-63. Urban planning (with Maxwell Fry and Jane Drew).
1951-64. The Capitol: High Court (1955), Secretariat (1958), Assembly (1964).
1964-68. Museum and art gallery.
1964-69. School of Art and Architecture.
1951-85. Monument of the "Open Hand".

**Projects built by Le Corbusier and his agency**
1945-52. Unité d'habitation, Marseilles.
1946-50. Claude et Duval factory, Saint-Dié, Vosges, France.
1948-55. Unité d'habitation, Rézé-les-Nantes, Loire-Atlantique, France.
1949. Curutchet house, La Plata, Argentina.
1950-55. Chapel of Notre-Dame-du-Haut (with André Maisonnier), Ronchamp, Haute-Saône, France.
1951-52. Cabanon, Cap-Martin, Alpes-Maritimes, France.
*Ahmedabad, Gujarat, India.*
1951-54. Millowners Association Building.
1951-56. Villas Sarabhai and Shodan.

1951-55. Maisons Jaoul, Neuilly-sur-Seine, Hauts-de-Seine, France.
1952-57. Aéro-club de Doncourt, Meurthe-et-Moselle, France.
1953-59. Pavillon du Brésil (with Lucio Costa), at the Cité universitaire de Paris.
1953-61. Monastery of Sainte-Marie-de-la-Tourette, Eveux-sur-Arbresle, Rhône, France.
1955-68. Cultural center and stadium, Firminy, Loire, France.
1956-63. Unité d'habitation, Briey-en-Forêt, Meurthe-et-Moselle, France.
1956-58. Unité d'habitation, Charlottenburg, Berlin.
1957-67. Unité d'habitation, Firminy, Loire, France.
1959. Museum of Western Art (with the Japanese architects Maekawa and Sakakura), Tokyo.
1960-62. Kembs-Niffer tidal gate (with Alain Tavès), Haut-Rhin, France.
1960-63. Carpenter Center for Visual Arts, (with José Luis Sert), Harvard University, USA
1963-67. Centre Le Corbusier-Heidi Weber, Zurich.

Death of Le Corbusier on August 27, 1965 in Cap-Martin, Alpes-Maritimes, France.

**Le Corbusier's grave at Roquebrune.**

# Bibliography


## Archives

*Carnet La Roche, 1922,* Gallimard/Electa, Paris, Milan, 1996.
*L'Esprit nouveau*, 8 volumes, Da Capo Piero, NewYork, 1968/1969.
*Le Corbusier. Œuvres complètes*, 8 volumes, rééd. Birkhäuser V/A, Bâle, Boston, Berlin, 1996.
*Le Corbusier. Carnets*, 4 volumes, The Architectural History Foundation, New York, 1981-1982, and Herscher/Dessain & Tolra, Paris, 1981-1984.
*The Le Corbusier Archive,* 32 volumes, edited by Allen Brooks, Garland Publishing Co/Fondation Le Corbusier, New York, Paris, 1982-1984.
*Voyage d'Orient. Carnets*, Fondation Le Corbusier/Electa Le Moniteur, Milan, 1987.

## Le Corbusier's main writings

*Aircraft*, The Studio, London, 1935, Trefoil/Adam Biro, Paris, 1987.
*Almanach d'architecture moderne*, Éditions Crès & Cie, Paris, 1925, new ed. Connivences, Paris, 1987.
*L'Art décoratif d'aujourd'hui*, Éditions Crès & Cie, Paris, 1925, new ed. Arthaud, Paris, 1980 and Flammarion, coll. Champs, 1996.
*La Charte d'Athènes*, Plon, Paris, 1943, new ed. Minuit, Paris, 1957 and Le Seuil, Paris, 1971.
*Essential Le Corbusier: L'Esprit Nnouveau Articles,* Butterworth Architecture, 1998.
*Une maison, un palais*, Éditions Crès & Cie, Paris, 1928, new ed. Connivences, Paris, 1989 and Altamira, Paris, 1994.
*Manière de penser l'urbanisme*, L'Architecture d'aujourd'hui, Paris, 1946, new ed. Denoël/Gonthier, Paris, 1977.
*Le Modulor*, L'Architecture d'aujourd'hui, Boulogne 1950, and *Le Modulor 2, la parole est aux usagers*, L'Architecture d'aujourd'hui, Paris, 1955, new ed. 1991.
*Une petite maison*, Girsberger, Birkhäuser, Bâle, 1996.
*Le Poème de l'angle droit,* Tériade, Paris, 1955, new ed. Fondation Le Corbusier/Connivences, Paris, 1989.
*Poésie sur Alger*, Falaize, Paris, 1950, new ed. Connivences, Paris, 1989.
*Précisions sur l'état présent de l'architecture et de l'urbanisme*, Éditions Crès, Paris, 1930, new ed. Altamira, Paris, 1994.
*Quand les cathédrales étaient blanches,* Plon, Paris, 1937, new ed. Denoël/Gonthier, Paris, 1977.
*Les Trois Établissements humains,* Denoël, Paris, 1945, new ed. Minuit, Paris, 1959.
*Urbanisme*, Éditions Crès & Cie, Paris, 1925, new ed. Arthaud, Paris, 1980 and Flammarion, coll. Champs, 1994.
*Vers une architecture*, Éditions Crès & Cie, 1923, new ed. Arthaud, Paris, 1977 and Flammarion, coll. Champs, Paris, 1995
*La Ville Radieuse*, L'Architecture d'aujourd'hui, Boulogne, 1935, new ed. Vincent Fréal, Paris, 1964.

## Collective works

*Architecture in India*, Electa/Le Moniteur, Milan, 1985.
*Le Corbusier. Une encyclopédie*, edited by de Jacques Lucan, éditions du Centre Georges Pompidou/CCI, Paris, 1987.
*Le Corbusier. Architect of the Century*, Arts Council of Great Britain, London, 1987.

## Books on Le Corbusier

BENTON (Tim), *Les Villas de Le Corbusier 1920-1930*, Philippe Sers, Paris, 1984.
BESSET (Maurice), *Le Corbusier*, Skira, Geneva, 1987.
CURTIS (William J. R.), *Le Corbusier Ideas and Forms*, Phaidon, London, 1986.
FRAMPTON (Kenneth), *Le Corbusier*, Hazan, Paris, 1997.
JENGER (Jean), *Le Corbusier: Architect, Painter, Poet*, Discoveries, Harry N Abrams, 1996.
PETIT (Jean), *Un couvent de Le Corbusier*, Minuit, Paris, 1961, new ed. 1990.
RAGOT (Gilles) and DION (Mathilde), *Le Corbusier en France. Réalisations et projets*, Electa/Le Moniteur, Paris, 1987, new ed. 1992 and 1997.
SBRIGLIO (Jacques), *L'unité d'habitation de Marseille*, éditions Parenthèses, Marseille, 1992 ; *Immeuble 24 N.C. et Appartement Le Corbusier*, Fondation Le Corbusier/Birkhäuser, Bâle, Boston, Berlin, 1996 ; *Villa La Roche, villa Jeanneret*, Fondation Le Corbusier/Birkhäuser, Bâle, Boston, Berlin, 1996.
VOGT (Adolf, Max), *Le Corbusier, the Noble Savage: Toward an Archaeology of Modernism*, MIT Press, 1998.

## Acknowledgements

This work would not have been possible without the help and cooperation of the following institutions and individuals to whom the authors wish to express their gratitude:
Mme Evelyne Tréhin, director of the Fondation Le Corbusier, Paris; the Ebel company and Mme Perret-Sgualdo, La Chaux-de-Fonds, Switzerland; the municipality of Corseaux, Switzerland; M. Jacques Hondelatte, architect in Bordeaux; M. Guarrigue, architect in Pessac; M. Veyssière-Pommot, curator of the villa Savoye, Saint-Germain-en-Laye; M. Maurice Besset, art critic, Geneva, Switzerland; Mme Deroche, Director pavillon suisse, Cité universitaire, Paris; the Salvation Army in Paris; M. Keller, M. Moreau and M. Viallot of the Unité d'habitation in Marseilles; Mr. Sarabhai in Ahmedabad, India; œuvre Notre-Dame-du-Haut in Ronchamp; Lord Palumbo in London; M. Laurent Duport in Nîmes and M. Makli in Neuilly-sur-Seine; Prior Brice Olivier, Father Antoine Lion and M. Pierre-Emmanuel Ansart at the monastery of la Tourette; the city of Roquebrune-Cap-Martin; Patricia Dinev, Paris.

## Photo credits

Fondation Le Corbusier: photos p. 6, 16, 27, 65, 74, back cover; plans and drawings p. 10-11, 16-17, 26-27, 34-35, 43, 52-53, 64, 74-75, 82-83, 88-89, 96-97, 110-112, 128-129, 142-143, 150-151, 169, 182
Photos Lucien Hervé, Paris: p. 113, 182-183
Photos René Burri/Magnum Photos: p. 88, 168
Photo Bodo Rasch Archives: p. 42
Photo IGN – Paris 1998: p. 130-131
Photos Anriet Denis-Adob Design: front cover, p. 2, 9, 12-15, 19-25, 28-33, 36-41, 44-51, 54-63, 76-81, 84-87, 90-95, 98-109, 114-127, 132-141, 144-149, 152-167, 170-181, 184-189, 191
Private collection: front cover (Le Corbusier's profile)

Printed in Italy
by Grafiche Zanini - Bologna